Antique Country Furniture
of
North America
and details of its construction

John G. Shea

PRENTICE HALL PRESS

New York   London   Toronto   Sydney   Tokyo

Other John G. Shea Books

The American Shakers and their Furniture

Woodworking for Everybody

Contemporary Furniture

Colonial Furniture Making for Everybody

Plywood Working for Everybody

Pennsylvania Dutch and their Furniture

Copyright © 1975 by Prentice Hall, Inc.

Published in 1986 by Prentice Hall Press
A Division of Simon & Schuster, Inc.
Gulf + Western Plaza
One Gulf + Western Plaza
New York, NY 10023

Originally published by Van Nostrand Reinhold Company Inc.

PRENTICE HALL PRESS is a trademark of Simon & Schuster, Inc.

Library of Congress Cataloging-in-Publication Data

Shea, John Gerald.
    Antique country furniture of North America.

    Bibliography: p.
    Includes index.
1. Furniture—United States.   2. Antiques—United
    States.   3. Furniture—Canada.   4. Antiques—Canada.
1. Title
Nk2405.S47   749.2′1   75-9118
ISBN 0-671-61058-9

Manufactured in the United States of America

10 9 8 7 6 5 4 3 2

Contents

Preface

The ambitions of this work involved the exploration of all elementary *antique-country-furniture* designs used in North America during the past four hundred years. The definition of *"country furniture,"* in its present popular context, excludes all furniture of sophisticated design. This rules out the more ornate mahogany, inlaid, veneered, carved and complex-shaped period pieces. Thus, from the start, the lines were sharply drawn to deal only with provincial, handmade designs — generally of simple solid-wood construction.

Considering the multiplicity of nationalities and ethnic influences that produced such furniture, it seemed desirable to break the book down into separate subchapters dealing specifically with each influence. But the scope and comprehensiveness of treatment required for each influence posed separate problems. Indeed, dozens of books have been written on each of them. Still, I did not wish to fall into the trap suggested by a Texas friend, who remarked that most books of antiques failed to consider designs that originated *"west of the Hudson River."* of course, I intended to penetrate far *"west of the Hudson River."* But after considerable study, I ultimately learned that there was not too much distinctive material available in some western regions.

So, in the course of research, hundreds of letters were sent to curators of *all* significant United States museums as well as those of Canada. Thus all regions of North America were invited to contribute material relating to their historical holdings. It was reasoned that state and regional museums were in the best position to advocate recognition of noteworthy work performed in their areas.

The results of these hundreds of inquiries were not too satisfactory. For instance, it was interesting to observe the number of western and midwestern museums holding antique furniture which had originated in New England. (Of course, it is logical to assume that much early furniture was moved from east to west by pioneering settlers.) Also, a preponderance of awkward, primitive pieces emerged from many regional museums. Most of these pieces were noteworthy only because of their historical relationship to the settlement of the areas where they originated. Looked at separately, in comparison with other country designs coming from other regions, they simply did not qualify.

At all times the criteria of good design and good taste determined the selection of the furniture shown. It would seem that *antiquity* alone should not suffice to qualify for current interest furniture which is poorly designed. Indeed, some of the drab designs housed in museums throughout this country as authentic "antiques" would better serve aesthetic purposes if they had passed into oblivion along with their makers.

Thus the original ambition of having *all* regions and *all* nationalities represented in this book had to be modified. This was because of the quality of material available and the limitations of book space. However, all important European influences are fully described. By linking the expression of regional European designs a clearer and more definitive representation seemed possible.

In this way the separation of English-speaking contributors include the work of English, Irish, Scotch and Welsh craftsmen who came to populate New England and other English colonies. *Spanish Colonial* also implies consideration of the work of other nationalities of the Mediterranean and southern Europe. *French Canadian* sketches the provincial expression of France. *Dutch Colonial* and *Pennsylvania German* also represent the European midlands, while *Norwegian American* deals with Scandinavian influences.

So, this book endeavors to highlight the principal ethnic and religious cultures which influenced the development of American country furniture. By way of bicentennial observation and to trace the original discoveries and explorations of the various nationalities who came to settle in America, background information is offered on the early colonization of the United States and Canada.

In order to determine the proper proportions of contents, an overall evaluation had to be made of the significance of various influences. Thus the number of pages devoted to *New England Colonial* exceeds that of *Spanish Colonial*, because the furniture produced in early New England is uniquely designed and has come to be more widely recognized and commonly used than that which remains to remind us of our Spanish heritage. By the same token, when considering contributions of religious cultures, it became abundantly evident that because of its graceful styling and functional attributes the furniture craftsmanship of the American Shakers exceeded in importance that of many other religious cultures. Hence, an increased amount of space was devoted to its presentation.

For the final chapter of measured drawings of country classics, a random selection was made of popular country antiques, spanning several influences. It is hoped that this chapter may help serious students and craftsmen to reproduce some of these venerable country classics.

John G. Shea
Greenwich, Connecticut
August 2, 1975

Woodworkers' Conversion Table

Imperial inches	Metric millimeters	Woodworkers' parlance (mm.)	Metric millimeters	Imperial inches	Woodworkers' parlance (in.)
¹⁄₃₂	0.8	1 bare	1	0.039	¹⁄₁₆ bare
¹⁄₁₆	1.6	1½	2	0.078	¹⁄₁₆ full
⅛	3.2	3 full	3	0.118	⅛ bare
³⁄₁₆	4.8	5 bare	4	0.157	⁵⁄₃₂
¼	6 4	6½	5	0.196	³⁄₁₆ full
⁵⁄₁₆	7.9	8 bare	6	0.236	¼ bare
⅜	9.5	9½	7	0.275	¼ full
⁷⁄₁₆	11.1	11 full	8	0.314	⁵⁄₁₆
½	12.7	12½ full	9	0.354	⅜ bare
⁹⁄₁₆	14.3	14½ bare	10	0.393	⅜ full
⅝	15.9	16 bare	20	0.787	¹³⁄₁₆ bare
¹¹⁄₁₆	17.5	17½	30	1.181	1³⁄₁₆
¾	19.1	19 full	40	1.574	1⁹⁄₁₆ full
¹³⁄₁₆	20.6	20½	50	1.968	1¹⁵⁄₁₆ full
⅞	22.2	22 full	60	2.362	2⅜ bare
¹⁵⁄₁₆	23.8	24 bare	70	2.755	2¾
1	25.4	25½	80	3.148	3⅛ full
2	50.8	51 bare	90	3.542	3⁹⁄₁₆ bare
3	76.2	76 full	100	3.936	3¹⁵⁄₁₆
4	101.4	101½	150	5.904	5¹⁵⁄₁₆ bare
5	127.0	127	200	7.872	7⅞
6	152.4	152½	300	11.808	11¹³⁄₁₆
7	177.5	178 bare	400	15.744	15¾
8	203.2	203 full	500	19.680	19¹¹⁄₁₆
9	228.6	228½	600	23.616	23⅜ bare
10	254.0	254	700	27.552	27⁹⁄₁₆
11	279.5	279½	800	31.488	31½
12	304.8	305 bare	900	35.424	35⁷⁄₁₆
18	457.2	457 full	1,000	39.360	39⅜ bare
24	609.6	609½			
36	914.4	914½			

Acknowledgments

For their courteous cooperation in furnishing photographs and information, separately identified and credited in this book, the author wishes to thank the following museums and historical sources:

The Agnes Etherington Art Center, Queen's University, Kingston, Ontario, Canada.

The American Museum in Britain, Bath, England.

The Atlanta Historical Society, Atlanta, Georgia.

The Baker Furniture Museum, Holland, Michigan.

The Carlen House Museum, Mobile, Alabama.

De Saisset Art Gallery and Museum, University of Santa Clara, Santa Clara, California.

The First Ironworks Association, Saugus, Massachusetts.*

Fruitlands Museums, Harvard, Massachusetts.

Greenfield Village & Henry Ford Museum, Dearborn, Michigan.

The Henry Francis du Pont Winterthur Museum, Winterthur, Delaware.

Historic St. Augustine Preservation Board, St. Augustine, Florida.

The Hitchcock Chair Company, Riverton, Connecticut.

Index of American Design, National Gallery of Art, Washington, D.C.

The Ipswich Historical Society, Ipswich, Massachusetts.*

Little Norway Museum, Blue Mounds, Wisconsin.

Longfellow's Wayside Inn, Sudbury, Massachusetts.

The Maine State Museum, Augusta, Maine.

The Metropolitan Museum of Art, New York, New York.

The Montreal Museum of Fine Arts, Montreal, Canada.

Musée du Quebec, Quebec, Canada.

The National Gallery of Canada, Ottawa, Canada.

The National Museum of Man, Ontario, Canada.

New York State Museum, Albany, New York.*

The Norwegian American Museum, Decorah, Iowa.

The Philadelphia Museum of Art, Philadelphia, Pennsylvania.*

The Shaker Museum, Old Chatham, New York.*

The Shaker Museum, Sabbathday Lake, Maine.*

Sleepy Hollow Restorations, Tarrytown, New York.

Upper Canada Village, Morrisburg, Ontario, Canada.

Wadsworth Atheneum, Hartford, Connecticut.*

Warren County Historical Museum, Lebanon, Ohio.*

Winedale Inn, The University of Texas at Austin.

Photographs supplied from previous books.

I HISTORICAL BACKGROUND OF REGIONAL DESIGNS

Reception room of restored early 19th century Spanish mission at Santa Barbara, California, shows heavy plastered adobe walls, original floor tiles and beams and ceiling constructed of native pine. Furniture and accessories were restored from designs produced by Indian neophytes under the direction of Spanish mission padres. (*Courtesy, Index of American Design*)

Spanish Colonial

Who *really* discovered America? This formidable accomplishment has been variously ascribed to the Scandinavians, the Greeks, the Buddhists, the Etruscans, the Hindus, the Japanese — and even the Welsh. And because of the proximity of the Bering Straits, which separate Siberia from Alaska by only a few miles, the Russians contend that they set foot on the North American continent centuries before anyone else appeared.

But for all effective and enduring purposes, the "discovery" of America in 1492 by Christopher Columbus, an Italian in the employ of Spain, seems to have resolved the issue. For thereafter, America became rapidly settled, and in 1493, 1498 and 1502, Columbus returned to establish Spanish claims to territory in the New World.

Ironically, Columbus, who had set out to circumnavigate the globe in order to find new and less dangerous routes to the Orient, never learned that he had failed to accomplish that mission. From his voyages he brought back to Spain samples of exotic plants, birds of brilliant plumage and *some* gold. He also brought back a few native "Indians" — so-called because he believed he had discovered a new route to the East Indies. All of these things, Columbus believed, represented the treasures of the East.

The first settlement of the Spanish in America was made in Panama by Alonzo de Ojeda in 1508. The island of Jamaica was colonized by the Spanish in 1509; Cuba, in 1511 and Puerto Rico, the Greater Antilles, Central America and Peru, shortly thereafter.

In 1513, Ponce de Léon explored Florida. He was followed in 1541 by De Soto, who penetrated into this territory and continued to explore the lands lying between Florida and the Mississippi River. The first permanent settlement on land now part of the continental United States was made at St. Augustine, Florida, in 1565.

Also in 1513, Balboa crossed the Isthmus of Panama to first sight the Pacific Ocean. Meanwhile, another Spaniard, Cortez, conquered the Aztecs of Mexico. And in 1528, Pizarro subdued the Inca tribes of Peru.

Mexico City then became the base for further Spanish expansion on the mainland. Thus "New Spain" came to include Mexico and all southwestern and western areas of North America. The Spanish were the first to explore and colonize vast regions of the present United States, moving from Florida, the Gulf states, the islands of the Caribbean and up from Mexico into the Pacific west coast. By 1600, Spanish navigators had extended their voyages southward as far as Chile and Argentina.

In 1493 a Papal Bull confirmed Spain's right to the New World. The religious purpose was to spread Christianity among the heathens of the new land. But in their priorities the Spanish placed "gold and glory" above "gospel" — as

Armario, built in Cataluna, Spain, around 1750, has four paneled doors and is fitted with shelves inside. This large walnut cupboard typifies early Spanish designs imported to America. (*Courtesy, Historic St. Augustine Preservation Board*)

witnessed by their cruel treatment of the Aztecs and the Incas. Indeed, in their pursuit of "gold and glory" the aggressive Spanish murdered entire tribes to pilfer their gold and other precious materials, which they brought back to enrich the coffers of Spain.

Spanish exploration and domination over vast areas of North and South America continued until 1588, when the Spanish Armada was battered and sunk by the British. Then, denied supremacy of the seas, Spain's expansion of America's "New Spain" was halted. Thereafter, the Atlantic Ocean became an open highway for the Dutch and French — and, most of all, for the English.

During the next two hundred years, Spain retained her hold on vast portions of the present United States, including the present states of Arizona, Texas, California and New Mexico. Here, she developed an outpost economy and military government throughout a territory which was half the size of Europe. The plundering practices of the conquistadors gave way to the peaceful and industrious life of the rancher, with the result that large cattle ranches were established by the Spanish in Mexico and the southwestern regions.

This is a mid-18th century copy of a 17th century Spanish dining table. The top consists of one solid board supported by massive volute legs and wrought-iron tie-rods. In background is an early Spanish chair, paneled indoor shutter and cupboard. (*Courtesy, Historic St. Augustine Preservation Board*) See measured drawing, page 152.

Mesa pequeña, or small service table, was imported from Castile, Spain, around 1790. This is a simple, one-drawer table with chip-carved front. The top consists of one very wide board. (*Courtesy, Historic St. Augustine Preservation Board*) See measured drawing, page 149.

Early 17th century Spanish *vargueño*, or traveling desk, was intricately paneled and inlaid. It has locked drawers and compartments and carrying handles at each end. (*Courtesy, De Saisset Art Gallery, University of Santa Clara*)

Spanish Missions in California

Although it had not been colonized, the present state of California was part of New Spain. Indeed, the Spanish governors, luxuriating in their places in Mexico, had no desire to colonize the north until King Charles III of Spain received word that the Russians were invading Monterey Bay. Actually, the Russians had no designs on occupying the California coast; they had been drawn there in pursuit of sea otters — the pelts of which were highly prized in trade.

But King Charles III, convinced that the Russians were intent on establishing New World colonies in upper California, ordered military expeditions from Mexico to build a chain of forts and to secure the coast of California against any such invasion.

In accordance with the Spanish practice of sending priests along to "pacify" the natives during forays into unsettled territories, in 1768 Father Junipero Serra accompanied Captain Gaspar de Portola on his expedition into upper California. Father Serra was a wise and kindly man of God. In fact, he reversed the ferocity of the conquistadors by gently converting the Indians to the faith — and by establishing enduring missions at each place along the California coast where Spanish forts were erected. All in all he built twenty-one missions — many of which still remain to remind Californians of their Spanish heritage.

Architecture and Furniture

Early Spanish dwellings in America were naturally influenced by the Spanish Renaissance architecture which prevailed in that country between the years 1492 and 1650. This reflected the influence of earlier Moorish work with its rich decoration of patios, galleries, doorways and windows. The Spanish home was built around a central patio or court, with all the rooms a simple rectangular shape. In America, they were usually built of masonry (adobe) and fashioned in broad, low, ranch-type configurations. Of course, the homes of the aristocracy were more elaborate and usually incorporated features of architecture and furnishings imported from the homeland.

Decorative use of large nail heads, together with hand-tooled leather, distinguishes this early Spanish California chair. Mission chair, at right, from the late 18th century, is copiously hand-carved. Note variety of carved patterns and notched-type finials typical of early Spanish work. Santa Barbara mission bench, below, is believed to have been built around 1820 by Indian neophytes under direction of Spanish mission padres. *(Courtesy, Index of American Design)*

Painted chests were among the first articles brought into the American southwest from Mexico. Ornately painted traveling chests, such as the one shown here, were made in small sizes so they could be carried by pack mules. (*Courtesy, Index of American Design*)

This Spanish wooden chest was made around 1750. The front is decorated with chip-carved rosettes in the Moorish style. Note dovetailed construction and large wrought-iron lock. (*Courtesy, Historic St. Augustine Preservation Board*)

Animated painted designs of this early New Mexico chest front typifies primitive motifs used to decorate some antique Spanish chests. As means of transportation improved, Spanish chests were made larger. (*Courtesy, Index of American Design*)

One of the most striking features of early Spanish houses was produced by the use of hand-wrought ironwork for practical and decorative purposes. Superb iron grilles were used at the windows and openings. Handsome wrought-iron handrails were also an important decorative feature. Other built-in decorations found in the Spanish house were rich and colorful and most impressive when viewed in contrast to the plain, smooth, white plaster walls.

The use of colorful tiles for roofs, flooring and other purposes also contributed to the distinctiveness of the Spanish home.

Spanish furniture of the sixteenth and seventeenth centuries was also influenced by the Renaissance and traditional Moorish styles. Walnut was the most popular furniture wood, with oak, chestnut and pine also frequently used. Cedar and exotic fruitwoods sometimes supplemented other choices.

Unlike their contemporaries in other countries, the Spanish seemed content with only a limited number of different furniture pieces. Basic designs included chairs, stools, benches, tables, chests, beds, *vargueños* (traveling desks) and cupboards.

Both in Spain and in Spanish America, craftsmen employed intricate methods to decorate their furniture. Delicate inlaid work, combined with elaborate carving, painting and gilding, was used to enrich surface areas. The carving was frequently of the distinctive "chip" variety.

Otherwise, the Spanish were superb metalists, unsurpassed at producing elaborate and delicate wrought-iron work. Frequently, the wrought-iron bracing of table legs, chairs, benches and other pieces contributed significantly to their pleasing design.

Also, the Spanish, with their love of leather and their unsurpassed ability to work with it, produced finely tooled seats for chairs and the surfaces of chests. These, combined with decorative metal nail heads, driven in side by side along the edges — or forming geometric surface designs — created the distinctively different Spanish furniture. The derivation of these distinctive designs from earlier Moorish influences remains obvious — even in today's output of Spanish furniture.

Seventeenth century Spanish gate-leg table, made of pine and walnut, displays distinctive Spanish turning and decorative treatment of scrolled aprons. The drawer runs the width of the table. (*Courtesy, Historic St. Augustine Preservation Board*)

Sturdy early California chest of drawers was influenced by Spanish design. Note how rails are through-tenoned to secure ultimate strength of construction. (*Courtesy, Index of American Design*)

New England — returned to England! Cozy corner of 17th–18th century Conkeys' New England Tavern, now reconstructed at the American Museum, Bath, England, contains typical early American bow-back and comb-back Windsor chairs and oval-top tavern table. Doll's cradle and child's rocker, shown at left, demonstrate the early colonists' concern for making furniture suitable for children. (*Courtesy, The American Museum in Britain, Bath, England*)

New England Colonial

As early as 1497–1498, England made claim to North American territory because of voyages of discovery and exploration made to this continent by John Cabot. Cabot, like Columbus, was an Italian who had settled in England in 1470 and became a naturalized citizen in 1476. He sailed on a voyage of discovery from Bristol, England, in 1497, under the authority of letters patent from King Henry VIII. Convinced, as was Columbus, that he had circumnavigated the globe, he discovered a region of North America which he believed to be the coast of China.

On returning to England with news of his discovery, Cabot was graciously received by the king and encouraged to continue his journeys. He then made a second voyage to America, during which he visited Labrador and the Gulf of St. Lawrence. Continuing southward, he cruised along the coast of New England as far as Cape Cod.

Accompanying Cabot on his first voyage was his son Sebastian, who later continued to explore the coast of North America. In 1517, Sebastian Cabot tried to find a northwest passage to the Orient. In so doing, he visited Hudson Bay and later explored the shores of Newfoundland. Eventually, he sailed south along the Atlantic coast as far as Florida.

In 1526, Sebastian Cabot entered the service of Spain. He then explored the coast of Brazil and the La Plata River. At several places he attempted to establish colonies. Returning to Spain in 1530, he stayed but a short while before going back to England. In this country he received a pension from King Edward VI in recognition of his earlier discoveries on behalf of England.

After returning to England, Sebastian Cabot prepared a series of maps and charts of parts of the New World he had discovered or explored. He was, in fact, the first to realize that entirely new continents had been discovered. As a result of his numerous voyages, he also improved the science of navigation by establishing new principles regarding variations of the mariners' compass.

Adventures of Sir Francis Drake

Thus, on the precedent of early voyages by the Cabots, England claimed parts of North America as her own. These claims were reinforced some years later by the marauding adventures of Sir Francis Drake.

In essence, Drake was a royally glorified pirate who made voyages to Guinea and the Gulf of Mexico to destroy Spanish ports and to plunder Spanish treasure ships in the West Indies. Since he was highly proficient at molesting and robbing the Spanish — and invariably returned to England with massive cargoes of Spanish treasure — Queen Elizabeth admired and rewarded him for his acumen. In fact, she equipped him with five small ships and a crew of one hundred and sixty-six men, with instructions to undertake a voyage to the South Seas via the Strait of Magellan.

Exquisitely carved and detailed small oak cabinet, marked "TH 1679," belonged to Thomas Hart of Lynnfield, Massachusetts. (*Courtesy, Winterthur Museum*)

The "Great Hall" of the historical Whipple House at Ipswich, Massachusetts, has the huge 17th century fireplace flanked by spinning wheel, stool and ladderback chairs. At the right, a dough box stands beside an unusually severe pine cupboard. A wooden churn peeks out from behind the comb-back Windsor chair, and the tavern table is set with pewter to serve the evening repast. (*Courtesy, Ipswich Historical Society*)

On this great adventure, Drake first went to the coast of Chile. Then, sailing north, he harassed and plundered every Spanish ship and port along the way. He continued to sail north to a region above San Francisco before casting out for the East Indies and returning to England. By this time his flagship, the *Golden Hind,* was loaded to the gunwales with foreign treasures — plundered mostly from Spanish merchantmen plying routes between Spain and the New World.

As a result of his highly lucrative adventures, Drake, the most celebrated buccaneer in history, was knighted by the Queen. And the Crown, as well as the merchants of England, were made profoundly aware of the vast treasures which were there to be extracted from America.

Start of English Colonization

Thus, in London, it was decided that discovery, exploration and colonization of America must be encouraged. Because of commercial rivalry between the shippers of London, two companies were organized — one from London and one from Plymouth.

In 1606, three ships, sailing under the aegis of the London Company, followed the southern route via the Azores and the Canary Islands to cruise the West Indies. They then went north, intent on settling a section between Spanish Florida and the French in Quebec. In April, 1607, they entered Chesapeake Bay. Penetrating inland, they followed what is now known as the James River and anchored off a wooded island which, in honor of the king, they named Jamestown. Unfortunately, this first English settlement in Virginia hardly survived its first winter. Thirty-nine members of the original company of one hundred and forty-four perished — and the remainder found little of the reputed "treasures" to be found in the New World.

Carved desk box, of 17th century New England origin, has hand-wrought iron hasp, lock and hinges. These were used to contain the colonists' family documents, books and writing materials. (*Courtesy, Fruitlands Museums*) See measured drawing, page 184.

Pilgrims and Puritans

But the experience at Jamestown convinced the English trading company that substantial returns could still be extracted from America through settlement of the land by sober and industrious people, such as the Pilgrims — a separatist religious cult which believed the faith of Christ had been corrupted by the Church of England.

Because of persecution produced by their "separatist" faith in England, the Pilgrims picked up and moved to Holland. But there, too, they felt strange living among people of a foreign land. So, they decided the best, and only, place for them to go was America.

While they were viewed with disfavor by the Crown, through the influence of friends the Pilgrims were finally sponsored by the Virginia Company. Their voyage to America was subsidized by a loan of 7,000 pounds. Thus, on September 16, 1620, the good ship *Mayflower,* with 149 people aboard, set sail for the New World.

What they headed for was Virginia, which, in the regional definition of the time, ran up the Atlantic coast to include the present state of New Jersey. But, because of inefficient navigation, the *Mayflower* ran north of Virginia by several

Large butterfly table with carved Bible box of 17th century origin. Butterfly tables of various sizes and proportions were widely made throughout New England. (*Courtesy, Longfellow's Wayside Inn*) See measured drawing, page 165.

Highly carved, two-drawer Hadley chest was made in Massachusetts toward the end of the 17th century. The design of these chests originated in England. (*Courtesy, Index of American Design*)

Early Plymouth Court cupboard is believed to have belonged to Thomas Prence, who became governor of Plymouth, Massachusetts, in 1634. Detailed decoration of this cupboard closely resembles similar cupboards made at the time in England. (*Courtesy, Wadsworth Atheneum*)

Chest Carving

Carved oak chest, from around 1660–80, was elaborately decorated with carved three-tulip panels and split-turned bosses painted black. While the tulip design was commonly used, other florid carving motifs, illustrated on these pages, included the acanthus leaf and variations of sunflower designs. Extensive use of such carving distinguished all chests made in New England during the early period of colonization. Such carving also appeared on English chests which brought the colonists' belongings to this country. (*Courtesy, Index of American Design*)

hundred miles and made her first landfall at Cape Cod, Massachusetts. Ultimately, they landed and set up a permanent settlement at Plymouth, Massachusetts.

After the first year, during which they suffered extreme hardship, the Pilgrims learned how to cope with their New England wilderness. At first they lived off the land and sea by fishing and hunting — and by bartering their produce with the Indians for native corn. However, they soon were able to produce their own crops and develop their own industries.

Two-drawer sunflower chest, made in Connecticut, 1660–1680, shows individuality of carved motifs. Drawers were added to chests early in the 17th century, but lidded, open chest compartment remained on top part of the structure. (*Courtesy, Index of American Design*)

Colonial kitchen, above, reconstructed from house built at Oxford, Massachusetts, around 1740, shows a pine and birch chair-table, a Windsor high chair and comb-back Windsor armchair. Against the back wall, a Connecticut Valley cupboard holds earthenware plates, pewter dishes and a small wooden bowl. (*Courtesy, Winterthur Museum*) Painted whitewood chest of drawers, below, originated in New England around 1690. Note thistle motif surmounted by crown. End panel is boldly painted with large tulip. (*Courtesy, Index of American Design*)

Meanwhile, another English religious group, the Puritans, also decided to take their faith to America. Unlike the Pilgrims, the Puritans did not desire to separate their faith from the Church of England. Rather, they wished to "purify" the English faith by ridding it of aspects of the Papist survival in its ritual and church government. They would go to America, they decided, and there restore the purity of the church. There they would build a "New England" on a purer and more godly scale.

Led by John Winthrop, a well-educated and aristocratic landowner, the Puritans sailed for America in March, 1630. Their four ships carried over five hundred men, women and children.

Winthrop believed that the new colonies should be established on a sound economic basis. Thus, while the Puritans were dedicated to the "purified" worship of God, it was also part of their credo that man's duty to God required him to use his talents to their fullest extent. In this way it was acknowledged that man's material success would constitute a sign of God's blessing.

Because of their industry and enterprise the Puritans prospered in New England. By the end of 1630, there were one thousand English settlers in the Commonwealth of Massachusetts — and, by 1640, around twenty-five thousand more had

Corner of kitchen at Longfellow's Wayside Inn contains an old spinning wheel and pewter cupboard of early 18th century origin. Note huge burl bowl on table and candle lanterns hanging from beam. (*Courtesy, Longfellow's Wayside Inn*) See measured drawing of cupboard, page 207.

Painted Guilford chest, above, made in Connecticut during the first half of the 18th century, displays flamboyant painted motifs rarely used in New England. *(Courtesy, Index of American Design)* New England painted chest, below, built in 1815, exhibits fine proportions and decorative details. *(Courtesy, Fruitlands Museums)* See measured drawing, page 189.

arrived to colonize new communities near Boston. Later they moved into Rhode Island and, by 1643, had settled west to the Connecticut River and south as far as Long Island. They also moved north into New Hampshire and Maine.

Within a relatively short number of years, New England became populated by the English. Numerous towns and cities, usually bearing English names, took root throughout the countryside, extending northward from Long Island Sound to the Canadian border and westward from Boston to Albany. By the time the American Revolution started in 1776, there were over two million English-speaking people residing in America — including those of New England and the southern English colonies.

Early New England Furniture

When, in 1620, the *Mayflower* made her stormy voyage to Plymouth, Massachusetts, her cargo included only basic human necessities:

there was little or no furniture. Indeed, the records indicate that space in her crowded hold was so limited that she carried only a few wood-cutting tools to help the Pilgrims in their grim task of hacking new homes out of the New England wilderness.

In the face of severe hardship and the struggle for survival, people had little concern for furniture. The earliest settlers at Plymouth and elsewhere simply bivouacked in the forests and improvised crudely built shelters to protect themselves. Their safeguards against the elements often were holes dug in the sides of hills and covered with bark lean-to roofs. "Furniture" was apt to be a tree stump, log or stone on which to sit beside the open fire.

But when permanent settlements were secured in the New World, artisans and tools to work the forest became available, and better homes were built. With these, native furniture also began to make its appearance.

The oldest New England table, from around 1650, was originally called a "table board and frame." Top and triple trestles are demountable. This table, a gift of Mrs. Russell Sage, is now in the Metropolitan Museum of Art. (*Courtesy, Index of American Design*) See measured drawing, page 151.

The old taproom at Longfellow's Wayside Inn. Here, the landlord welcomed travelers, and his wife cooked for her family and guests over an open hearth. Governor Carver chair, chair-table and other furniture are all of early New England origin. (*Courtesy, Longfellow's Wayside Inn*)

At first, the furniture made in New England was necessarily crude and severely functional. Then skillful use of the broad axe and adze and laborious pitsawing made it possible to obtain squared lumber from the abundant forests. Handmade boards and beams improved the construction of early homes and communal buildings and at the same time provided materials to make the distinctive American style of furniture, now called "New England Colonial."

Such furniture, as we know it today, is found in soft, honey-colored pine, maple and birch, with occasional examples in darker tones of wal-

nut and cherry. Although such woods grew plentifully throughout New England and were widely used, the early craftsmen were not limited to these varieties alone. Indeed, any tree of good, straight growth could be made into furniture. But the back-breaking chores of felling, hewing and pitsawing understandably influenced the choice of softer woods offering less resistance to the crude tools of that period.

Pine was often used to make table tops, while harder woods were reserved for furniture parts subjected to tougher wear. Instead of applying the stains and luster finishes of today, the early

Turned tavern trestle table, which was built in Connecticut between 1670–1690, was light in weight and could be carried to the open hearth to serve the weary traveler. *(Courtesy, Wadsworth Atheneum)* See measured drawing, page 162.

Delicately turned small butterfly table is of early 18th century origin. The turning, which is quite different from that of other examples, demonstrates the individuality of early New England craftsmen. *(Courtesy, Longfellow's Wayside Inn)* See measured drawing, page 164.

This beautifully turned gate-leg table, of late 17th century origin, was a gift of Mrs. Russell Sage. *(Courtesy, Metropolitan Museum of Art)*

Exquisite, functional design of this 17th century gate-leg trestle table, a gift of Mrs. Russell Sage, may explain the enduring popularity of many early New England antiques. *(Courtesy, Metropolitan Museum of Art)*

furniture maker often scrubbed his handiwork and let time enrich the raw wood with darker tones. As an alternative, he would sometimes cover his product with crusty coats of paint.

Influences of the Old Country

In their way of living the New England colonists were still Englishmen only separated from their homeland by the Atlantic Ocean. Naturally, they brought with them the customs and habits of home — and their early homes and furniture reflected influences of the places from which they came.

Oblong-top tavern table, made with maple frame and pine top, was made in New England around the turn of the 18th century. (*Courtesy, Wadsworth Atheneum*) See measured drawing, page 167.

Oval-top tavern table, used for serving guests in early New England inns, was built early in the 18th century. (*Courtesy, Longfellow's Wayside Inn*) See measured drawing, page 166.

Many of the old carved chests, chairs, tables, benches and beds shown in this chapter have their counterparts in the antique furniture of England. In fact, the original colonial furniture of New England is, in some instances, almost identical to English country furniture of the seventeenth and eighteenth centuries. But, eventually, a distinctive American style evolved — a realization, perhaps, of the independent spirit as well as the special requirements of the early settlers.

During the seventeenth century, many different types of tables, chests and chairs originated throughout the New England colonies. Even during the earliest period when furniture designs often reflected the ponderous Gothic influences of Europe, some interesting modifications appeared on this side of the Atlantic. Traditional designs of the Old World frequently were revised to finer proportions and decorated with attractive carving and scrollwork which seemed to express the artistic emancipation of the American craftsman.

Early candlestand made provision for raising and lowering candles on maple shaft. Note cross-lap base construction. (*Courtesy, Longfellow's Wayside Inn*)

Early New England craftsmen excelled in the graceful application of curved scrolls and exquisitely turned shapes. They were masters of the *cyma curve* and applied it constantly to their furniture designs.

Construction

Native ingenuity played an important part in the construction of early New England furniture. Since metal for nails and screws was at first unobtainable and glue was virtually an unheard-of commodity, wooden furniture parts were fastened together of their own substance. This called for skillfully fitted dovetail and dado joints and for strong mortises and tenons held together with wooden pegs and wedged keys.

Fortunately, the pine trees of the New World grew to considerable girth. The breadth of antique table tops now displayed in our museums indicates that planks measuring as much as thirty inches wide were taken from these trees through industrious pitsawing, adzing and planing. This technique eliminated the need for joining boards together to form broad surfaces. Although the labor involved must have been formidable, the ingenious methods of construction employed by colonial craftsmen produced furniture which still stands strong and upright after centuries of wear.

Fireside view of the Hart Room at Winterthur Museum shows an ancient oak court cupboard attributed to Thomas Dennis, the master joiner of Ipswich, Massachusetts, and dated 1684. Near the corner is an early dowry chest. Beside the fireplace stands an old Governor Carver chair. In the foreground a carved wainscote chair of 17th century origin stands beside an early trestle-base gate-leg table. The joint stool in front of the table represents the most common seating form used in 17th century New England. *(Courtesy, Winterthur Museum)*

Governor Carver chairs, which originated in New England around 1650–1700, are distinguished by their three turned-back spindles of varied designs. There are a number of old Carvers in many museums, and they all seem to vary slightly in their proportions and details of turning. The one illustrated is a splendid example of early New England workmanship. (*Courtesy, Henry Ford Museum*) See measured drawing of alternate Carver design, page 137.

Winterthur reconstruction of 17th century room from a house built in 1684 at Essex, Massachusetts, shows Carver armchair and candlestand by the fireplace. In the corner hangs an old wall cupboard beside an ancient oak court cupboard. In the foreground a pine bench stands beside a stretcher-base table on which are wooden plates, burl bowl and pewter dish. (*Courtesy, Winterthur Museum*)

Excellent example of Windsor writing-arm comb-back chair of 18th century origin. This ingenious chair has two drawers: one under the writing counter and the other under the seat. It was probably reserved for the use of early scholars and statesmen. (*Courtesy, Henry Ford Museum*)

Cyma-scrolled pine cupboard is believed to have originated in New England early in the 18th century. This and the corner cupboard on opposite page exemplify colonial craftsmens' adroit application of cyma scrolls for the decoration of their work. As illustrated below, undulating cyma curves were applied to shape cabinet facings, chair and table aprons and other decorative uses. See measured drawing, page 204.

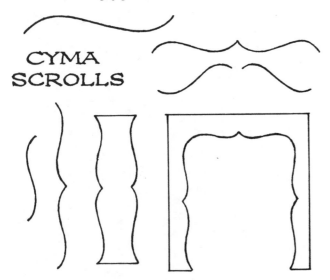

CYMA SCROLLS

Carved chests, court cupboards and Bible boxes, some of which are shown in this chapter, date back to the seventeenth century. Their development gives credence to the theory that *chests of drawers* evolved in this country from rudimentary, six-board sea chests. As prosperity prevailed, chest space eventually gave way to drawers and thus developed the chest of drawers as we know it today.

The Creative Colonials

Despite its humble origin, the design of early New England furniture shows inspired creativity — which distinguishes it as a style apart.

The enduring appeal of the sturdy old trestle tables, as exemplified by the venerable *triple trestle* of 1660 shown on page 21, focuses attention on the other large and small trestle tables shown throughout this chapter. The one on page 21 was first called a *table board and frame.* To save room space, it was made entirely demountable. The top is made of a single pine plank. It rests loosely on mortised trestles, which are strung along the center rail and held in place with removable keys.

The delightful variety of turned tables, such as the butterfly-trestle and gate-leg examples shown in this chapter, are almost exclusively of early New England design. Nowhere else in the world did these treasures blossom in such abundance and beauty.

The charm of colonial craftsmanship, seen in the original design of chests, stools, candlestands, hutches, sconces, wallboxes, racks, shelves, benches and the many other items shown on these pages, reveals the creative ability of the early craftsman — and offers insight into his artistic aspirations. For many of these designs are works of art. As such, they now transcend their original functions, which have long since become obsolete.

Sparsity of furniture in 17th century homes is evident in the East Bedroom of the Old Ironmaster's House at Saugus, Massachusetts. An ample oak chest, canopied bed, pegleg table and pine cradle complete the furnishing of this austere bedroom. (*Courtesy, First Ironworks Association*)

Scrolled corner cupboard, believed to have originated in Rhode Island around the turn of the 18th century, has exceptionally fine proportions and design. The open shelves were used to display prized pewter plates and dishes. (*Courtesy, Index of American Design*)

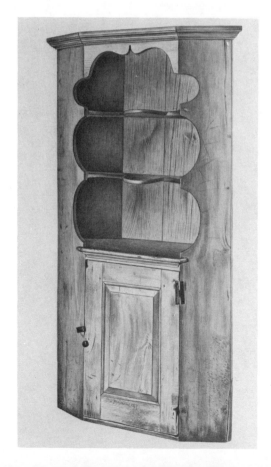

29

Old maps of North Eastern and Central America, engraved by Guillaume Delahaye in 1746, are shown above a Hudson Valley desk and early spindle-back Dutch armchair. A strong box rests on the desk, together with a large Dutch Bible. The Friesland clock and candlestand complete this interesting Dutch Colonial grouping. (*Courtesy, Sleepy Hollow Restorations*)

Dutch Colonial

Early in the seventeenth century, the United Provinces of the Netherlands claimed part of the North American continent, which they called "New Netherlands." This territory reached westward from the Atlantic Ocean to beyond the Delaware River and southward from Canada to Virginia. Conflict was caused when the English, soon afterward, commenced colonizing southern New England and the eastern part of Long Island. But the Dutch got there first because of Hudson's discovery of the "Great River" (Hudson River) in 1609, when he was in the employ of the Dutch East India Company and captain of the *Half Moon,* which flew the Dutch flag. Thus New Netherlands was first visited by Dutch sailors in 1610, and its coastline was charted by Dutch mariners during the following decade.

The Netherlands regarded this portion of North America as theirs by right of discovery and exploration. In fact, they assigned its management to the chartered Dutch West India Company. Between the years 1624 and 1664, this company prospered, sending Dutch settlers to the New World who energetically returned vast yields of furs, timber and other American products to the homeland.

But during these forty years, England surveyed Dutch activities in America with acrimony — and frequently notified the Netherlands that the Dutch were illegally occupying her lands. She based her claim on the fact that her mariners, the Cabots, had sailed along the coast as early as 1497–98. (Ironically, Hudson was an Englishman in the employ of the Dutch, while the Cabots were Italians in the employ of the English!) As an outcome of this controversy, Charles II gave New Netherlands to his brother James, Duke of York and Albany, who, in 1664, sent four armed frigates, under the command of Colonel Richard Nicolls, to capture New Amsterdam.

The governor of New Amsterdam, Director-General Petrus Stuyvesant, stubbornly refused to surrender the city — although it was feebly situated to withstand the military might of four fully armed British frigates. In fact, the burghers of New Amsterdam pleaded with Stuyvesant to yield and thus prevent bloodshed and destruction of their property. But it was not until the British warships directly confronted the Dutch fort, their guns trained broadside for its obvious destruction, that the obdurate Stuyvesant yielded.

English soldiers then debarked at the fort, lowered the Netherlands flag and raised the Union Jack. And, on September 8, 1664, Petrus Stuyvesant led his little garrison of Dutch soldiers out of Fort Amsterdam.

The Province was then made a colony of Great Britain — and New Amsterdam was renamed New York, in honor of the Duke of York. Other communities throughout the previously Dutch-held Province were also given English names or had their Dutch names anglicized.

Reconstructed Hardenberg bedroom, from an early Dutch home at Kerhonkson, New York, is dominated by a huge Dutch *kas* painted with grisaille motifs. Other furniture includes fiddleback chairs, a turned stool and a Hudson Valley cradle suspended from a turned trestle-foot frame. Against the back wall, beside the Friesland clock, is a Dutch *slaap banck*, or alcoved bed. (*Courtesy, Winterthur Museum*)

Slat-back armchair, probably made in New York around 1670–1700, shows elaborate Dutch decorative turning. (*Courtesy, Winterthur Museum*)

This sturdy Dutch table has turned rungs as well as turned legs. It is of early Hudson Valley origin. (*Courtesy, Sleepy Hollow Restorations*)

Made by Dutch craftsmen in the Hudson River Valley in the early eighteenth century, this lift-leaf table has massively turned legs — typical of the Dutch baroque style. Left leg splits in center to support leaf. (*Courtesy, Sleepy Hollow Restorations*) See measured drawing, page 168.

But the British takeover was short-lived. Exactly nine years later, England and Holland again engaged in militant conflict over who owned what territory in the New World. To implement their original claims, the Dutch sent over an armada of approximately two dozen warships to recapture New York in July 1673. On August 9, 1673, the city surrendered to the Dutch to again become part of New Netherlands — although the name of New York was changed to New Orange.

Paradoxically, the flip-flop of Dutch-English governments of New Netherlands came to an end with its return to English rule on February 9, 1674. This came about through the signing of the Treaty of Westminister between England and Holland. Under this treaty Holland received certain concessions in South America in return for England's repossession of Dutch territory on the continent of North America. Thus, while England ruled the land, the Dutch settlers remained to spread their influence and culture over substantial territories encompassed in the original Province of New Netherlands.

Early Dutch kitchen at Phillipsburg Manor displays sturdy chest-table, together with Dutch baroque chair (in background) and slat-back armchair. Both chairs were made in the Hudson Valley around 1700. Pegleg stool and wood box flank the fireplace beneath the Friesland clock. (*Courtesy, Sleepy Hollow Restorations*)

Continuation of Dutch Culture

By the time the English took over, the Dutch lifestyle was thoroughly implanted throughout the Province of New Netherlands. Houses typical of the traditional Dutch baroque style were constructed of stone or brick standing three or four stories tall. Farm houses were generally wooden-framed, although some were built of masonry. Often shingles, instead of clapboards, were used for covering both roof and sides of the house. Roofs were also thatched — although this ended in New Amsterdam with the proclamation of Governor Petrus Stuyvesant that thatched roofs must be banned because of their fire hazard.

In New Amsterdam, rows of neat brick houses, their facades shaped in stepped patterns in the typical Dutch architectural style, had bright red and blue tiled roofs. There was a raised stone doorstep at the front entrance. All buildings were scrubbed and kept spotlessly clean both inside and out.

The typically Dutch stepped-gable houses were built with a cellar and often a cellar kitchen. On the main floor there was a front and back room. There were also rooms on the second floor, with a garret and clock loft above.

Furniture, usually of the Dutch baroque style, was built more substantially and sometimes more ornately than that found in other colonies during the seventeenth century. Predominant in most homes was the Dutch *kas,* a huge wardrobe cabinet which, as shown on these pages, was intricately fashioned of massive panels and elaborate carving and was frequently vividly painted with flower or fruit motifs. This was the *pièce de resistance* in most early New Netherlands households, and it was so substantially built that many fine examples of the seventeenth century Dutch *kas* remain intact in our museums today.

The Dutch bed, called a *slaap banck,* was often built in as an integral part of the bedroom. It was more than a bed; rather, a curtained alcove sometimes completely built into the corner of a room with paneled sides and end — and with door enclosures to protect the sleeper from what was then regarded as *poisonous* night air. Many of these elaborate bed alcoves were imported from Holland by the more affluent Dutch settlers.

Early Dutch chairs varied from the true baroque types made with elaborate turning, carving and scrollwork (sometimes called *fiddleback chairs*) to the more conventional ladderback types of sizable proportions. Usually, chairs had seats woven of rush or splint. The type of turning employed varied from their New England counterparts to make them distinctively Dutch.

Tables, too, were sturdier than their early New England counterparts. Distinctive among these was a trestle type with a large storage case built below the top. Otherwise small and large gate-leg tables were built with plump turned legs. The girth of their legs frequently exceeded three inches. Small splay-legged tables with scrolled aprons were also frequently used. The spread of their slanted legs exceeded that of similar pieces made in other colonies.

Dutch cupboard, made around 1700, is colorfully decorated in the manner of the patroon school of painting. It has biblical scenes painted on the front and grisaille panels on the sides. This dominates the early Dutch dining room, which is otherwise furnished with baroque-style tables, chairs and stool. Note extreme slant of table legs. (*Courtesy, Sleepy Hollow Restorations*)

Collection of old furniture gracing the kitchen-dining room at Van Cortlandt Manor includes a country table dating from the second half of the 18th century. This exhibits a kind of structural bracing known only to the Hudson Valley. Furniture otherwise includes fiddleback chairs and typical fireplace accessories. Pewter cupboard, at the back, is not of early Dutch origin. (*Courtesy, Sleepy Hollow Restorations*)

Early New Netherlands homes were comfortably furnished with homey little knickknacks to remind the settlers of their original homes in Holland. Some had figured *storied glasses* in their windows and portraits, brought from the homeland — or painted locally — hanging on the walls. Usually small mirrors and a decorative Friesland clock lent an additional note of utility interest to their interiors.

Some of the more affluent New Netherlands burghers amassed considerable wealth in the New World and either imported their furniture from Holland or had pieces made in the Dutch style by local craftsmen. Thus, at the present time, some difficulty is experienced in distinguishing between early "Dutch Colonial" furniture made in America and those pieces originally imported from Holland.

Unusual plain turned gate-leg table is believed to be of Delaware Dutch origin, built in 1680. Observe the sturdy through-tenoned and pegged construction. (*Courtesy, Index of American Design*)

This close-up view of a corner at Phillipsburg Manor shows ornate Friesland clock together with open Dutch Bible and iron-bound strong box. Maps by cartographer S. Danville were engraved by Guillaume Delahaye in France in 1746. (*Courtesy, Sleepy Hollow Restorations*)

Kershner, Pennsylvania German Parlor, of the 18th century, reconstructed at Winterthur Museum, displays furniture and architectural details reminiscent of the German Renaissance period. Beside the walnut sawbuck table are *Moravian* splay-legged chairs as well as armchairs of early origin. In the corner stands a massive German *schrank*, while a painted dowry chest, dated 1774, rests on the floor between windows. On top of this, a Bible Box holds a German Bible printed in 1748. (*Courtesy, Winterthur Museum*)

Pennsylvania German

In 1681, William Penn received a charter from King Charles II of England to colonize the area of the New World now known as "Pennsylvania." Penn, a Quaker, opposed the religious beliefs of the Anglican Church as well as the Calvinist Puritans. As a result, the Quakers were persecuted in England and sought land in America where they could practice their faith in freedom.

William Penn, unlike his predecessors, encouraged people of other European nationalities to join the Quakers in seeking religious freedom in America. Thus, as well as Penn's Quakers, an influx of Scotch, Irish, French, Swedes and Germans settled in Pennsylvania. Among these, the German *Pietists,* who immigrated mostly from the Rhine Valley, came to this country.

The first German colonists went to Pennsylvania in 1683 and settled at Germantown, near Philadelphia. Later, they penetrated into the state and settled at such places as Lancaster, Bethlehem, Lititz and Nazareth. Eventually, they moved their families westward until they occupied nearly all regions of the state.

Early German immigrants were, for the most part, educated people who paid their own passage over from Europe. With them they brought tools and furniture and were able to pay for the land on which they settled. Some years later, however, poorer people of the Lutheran and German Reformed groups immigrated from the Rhine

Valley. These were too poor to pay for their passage. Called the *"Redemptioners,"* they agreed to work from four to seven years in the New World in voluntary servitude to pay off their debts of passage. After serving, they were granted fifty acres of farm land with tools to work their new property. The *Redemptioners* settled in the fertile valleys of the Lehigh, Susquehanna and Cumberland Rivers. Here, they established rich farms which prospered through succeeding generations.

From the beginning, the Germans in America existed as a people apart. They spoke a different language, which did not popularize them with the English and Scotch-Irish people of the new colonies. Also, their steadfast adherence to the religion and customs of the Old World caused further estrangement in their relations with English-speaking settlers. Moreover, they showed little interest in the social or political affairs of the colony and concentrated their energies almost wholly on the development of the finest farming regions in America.

The high mark of German immigration to America came around 1749–1754. At that time five thousand Germans arrived in this country each year. For the most part they maintained the same lifestyle as at home. Energetically and industriously they cultivated their Pennsylvania farms, advanced their domestic arts and pursued their religious beliefs in peace and prosperity.

Floral designs painted on pine dowry chest, above, identify it as an original made by Christian Selzer in 1784. Chest with drawers, below, is self-dated, indicating that it was made in Pennsylvania in 1794. (*Courtesy, Henry Ford Museum*)

On the walls of the Fraktur Room, reconstructed at Winterthur Museum, are examples of *fractur*, the medieval art of illuminated writing used to ornament important documents. The room paneling was taken from a stone farmhouse near Kutztown in Berks County, built in 1783 by David Hotenstein. Around the sawbuck table are walnut wainscot chairs made in Chester County. In the far corner a red and blue painted desk shows an interesting combination of the classical Philadelphia Chippendale style yielding to provincial folk-art decorations. To the left of the desk is a painted dowry chest of Berks County origin, decorated with unicorns and mounted horsemen. (*Courtesy, Winterthur Museum*)

Pennsylvania German hanging wall cupboard, of 18th century origin, is nicely detailed with elaborately scrolled apron. *(Courtesy, American Museum in Britain)* See measured drawing, page 175.

Plate rack, of early 19th century origin, shows typical Pennsylvania German detailing of fretwork with heart-shaped apertures and incised carving of circles enclosing five-pointed stars. *(Courtesy, American Museum in Britain)* See measured drawing, page 174.

Pennsylvania German Furniture

While most of the Germans who immigrated to Pennsylvania were farmers, there were also many skilled mechanics among them. These craftsmen created a distinctive Pennsylvania German style of furniture which was inspired largely by work they had previously performed in the old country.

Perhaps the most striking feature of all Pennsylvania German furniture is its flamboyant display of painted motifs. This is particularly true of the dowry chests shown on these pages. These were constructed as *hope chests* to hold stores of linen, with which every maiden was supposed to supply herself once she was able to finger a needle.

Usually, the dowry chest was painted a soft blue color. Over this were painted various motifs including vases of flowers, tulips, daisies, stars, birds, angels, unicorns and other devices. Many chests display the name of the owner and the date it was made, boldly inscribed on the front panel.

Impressive among the many Pennsylvania German furniture forms is the outsized cupboard — or *schrank* — which occupied much floor space in most early homes. The *schrank*, which was built along massive lines, could either be painted or plain-finished of walnut or cherry. Usually the painted versions were decorated with fruit or floral motifs.

Tables were made in the usual variety — some turned and others plain. Perhaps the most distinctive was the walnut sawbuck version shown on pages 38 and 43. The sawbuck ends were adroitly shaped and curved to modify the sturdy structure. Pierced by keyed-end tenons on the central rail, the table was so structurally durable that the original models, now well over two hundred years old, are still in useful condition.

Chairs of Pennsylvania German origin were, at first, substantially built to resemble the wainscot chairs of early New England. Later a variety of ladder-back and Windsor-type chairs made their appearance. *Arrow-back chairs,* so-called because their backs were made of shaved arrow-shaped spindles, were also commonly used.

Like much of the other Pennsylvania German furniture, chairs were also painted and decorated.

On a background of green, yellow or brown paint (sometimes "grained" to simulate natural wood markings) stenciled designs of fruit, flowers and birds were frequently applied.

In direct lineage of the work of the old country, a distinctive type of splay-legged chair, called a *Moravian chair* (see right), was widely used. This design, usually made with a pierced heart penetrating the back slab, simplified the chair-making process by using rungless peglegs for support.

As illustrated by the hanging cabinet and wall rack shown on page 42, the Pennsylvania Germans were also fastidious about the design of their incidental utility pieces. These always displayed an abundance of decorative detail, including elaborate scrollwork and pierced and painted features.

All in all, early Pennsylvania German furniture lacked the sophisticated elegance of furniture emanating from the centers of arts and culture at Philadelphia and elsewhere. This was plain

"Moravian" side chair was made in Pennsylvania following exactly the same design as earlier models made in Germany. (*Courtesy, Winterthur Museum*)

Walnut sawbuck table is beautifully proportioned and detailed to modify its massive size. Tables of this type were made by the Germans throughout Pennsylvania. The sturdy rails and key-tenoned construction warranted their enduring strength and practicality of design. (*Courtesy, Winterthur Museum*)

country furniture decorated to meet the tastes and needs of farmers and workmen living throughout the rural regions of Pennsylvania. But the elaborate use of paints and colorful motifs, together with distinctive turning and scrollwork, gave this furniture a feeling of its own. And thus it has emerged as distinctively "Pennsylvania German" — which separates it as a style apart from other furniture made in other colonies.

Unusual turning and scrollwork of this 18th century Pennsylvania German pine table make it particularly interesting. This is a small table, measuring 26″ high, 42″ long and 24″ wide. (*Courtesy, Index of American Design*)

The Pennsylvania Folk Art Room at Winterthur Museum brings together furniture and decorative objects made in Pennsylvania during the 18th and 19th centuries. On the shelves of the old pine dressers are earthenware plates and jars with *slip* and *sgraffito* decoration. The table is an unusual example of late 17th century gate-leg made in Pennsylvania. Armchairs beside the table are of early wainscot type. In the corner, another early armchair, chest and wall cupboard complete the picture. (*Courtesy, Wintherthur Museum*)

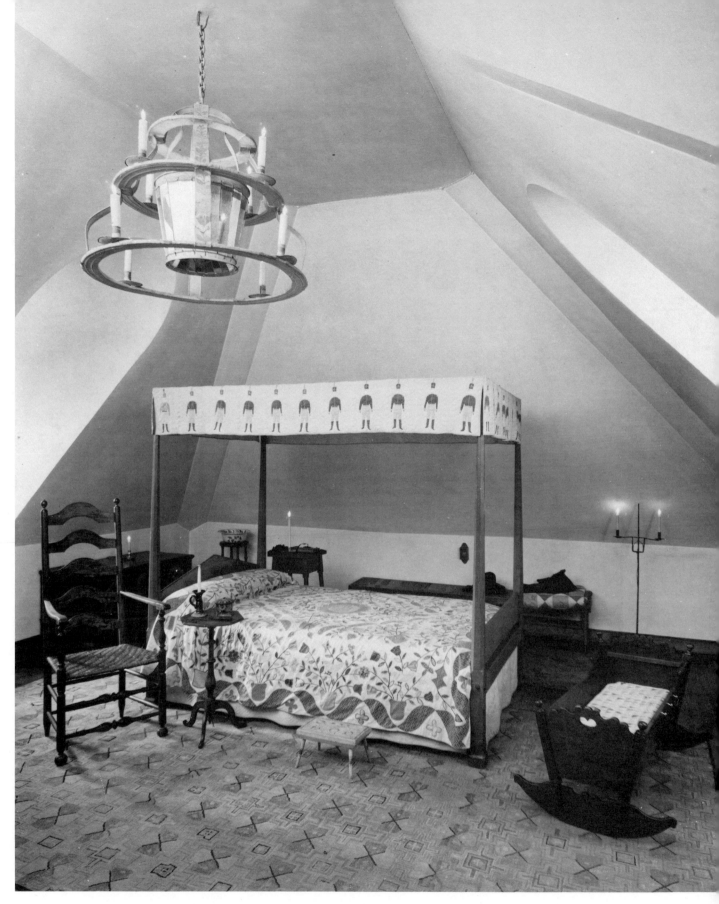

In this late 18th century Lebanon Bedroom, the furniture combines early and late forms. The pencil-post bed stands in the center of the room to clear the sloping ceiling. A green painted armchair represents a form of Pennsylvania slat-back popular throughout the region. Next to the chair stands an 18th century candlestand. In the foreground, at right, is a Pennsylvania walnut cradle, its scalloped end pierced with the popular heart motif. A large tin chandelier hangs above; the candlelight is reflected by strips of mirrored glass. (*Courtesy, Winterthur Museum*)

Typical French Canadian interior of the Maison du Calvet in Montreal shows massive stone walls and overhead rafters. In foreground, a chair-table flanks an 18th century diamond-point paneled chest and Louis XIII spiral-turned bed. The background displays an early 18th century two-tiered buffet, also with diamond-point panels. Across the corner stands a large armoire, chest of drawers and chairs. In the center, a 17th century Canadian gate-leg table, with typical Louis XIII turning, shares space with an early cradle. (*Courtesy, Montreal Museum of Fine Arts*)

French Canadian

French colonization of America was made possible by five explorers — Verrazano, Cartier, Champlain, Joliet and La Salle. It started in 1522, when the French captured a Spanish galleon containing a rich collection of gold and silver. Impressed by this valuable prize, King Francis I of France believed his plunder had come from the East Indies — and decided to seek a northwest passage thereto via a route which would penetrate through the northern regions of America. To undertake this journey, he chose another Genovese, Giovanni da Verrazano.

In 1524, Verrazano sailed first to the West Indies and then continued north along the coast seeking the elusive northwest passage. Eventually, he arrived at Newfoundland and the Strait of Belle Isle. He failed to discover a northern passage to the Indies but he did discover new territory, which he dutifully named "New France."

While King Francis I was dismayed by Verrazano's inability to find and penetrate an open route to the riches of the East, he did not abandon his dream. Some ten years later, in 1534, another French explorer by the name of Jacques Cartier sailed along the coast of North America. He made two voyages, during which he discovered and partially explored the St. Lawrence River. But still, he failed to find a new route to the Orient.

After these fruitless searches, the French became too preoccupied with their own internal disorders to pursue further exploration. So, for the next fifty years, discovery of latent wealth in Canada was left to traders and trappers.

Meanwhile the French *corsairs* continued to sail through the Bahamas and along the Florida coast. In fact, they attempted to found a colony in Florida. But they were repelled by the Spanish, who, in 1565, built the first of a line of forts at St. Augustine, which ultimately extended up into the Carolinas.

This might well have marked the end of French ambitions to colonize in America, had it not been for the prosperous growth of the Canadian fur trade. Toward the end of the sixteenth century it occurred to the French — as well as to other Europeans — that furs could be a more tangible asset than vague rumors of American gold.

So, in 1603, Samuel Champlain was sent out by France to trace the convolutions of the St. Lawrence, Saguenay, Ottawa and Richelieu Rivers. Champlain hoped that these rivers would lead to a vast inland sea. Because of his ability to get along peacefully with Indians, Champlain was able to establish a base at Quebec from which his explorations moved out among the friendly Algonquin and Huron tribes. He investigated the regions adjoining Lakes Ontario, Erie and Huron. It was Champlain who first organized the *coureurs du bois* (fur traders in the woods) and the *voyageurs* (traders in the plains), who ultimately carried French influence — and promoted the French fur trade from the St. Lawrence to the Rockies and from Hudson Bay to the Gulf of Mexico.

Unusual 17th century Canadian gate-leg table combines trestle-foot design with scrolled ends and rail. (*Courtesy, National Gallery of Canada*)

In 1625, the Jesuits sent missionaries to New France. They performed exceptionally well at making friends with the Indians and converting them to the Catholic faith. By 1671, the Jesuits had established missions throughout the French-held territory. In 1672, Father Marquette, a Jesuit, accompanied Louis Joliet on a voyage of exploration down the Mississippi River.

The final phase of French exploration went far beyond the Quebec wilderness. Under the leadership of Sieur de La Salle and with the help of Jesuit priests, exploration and settlement of the American hinterlands went south as far as the Gulf of Mexico. On April 9, 1682, La Salle claimed the entire Mississippi watershed in the name of King Louis XIV of France — calling the region "Louisiana" in his honor. Sometime later the French built the port of New Orleans.

X-trestle table, made at Quebec in the second half of the 18th century, combines practicality with adaptability. Top can be removed and X-trestles folded for storage when not in use. (*Courtesy, Agnes Etherington Art Center, Queen's University at Kingston, Ontario, Canada*)

This handsome diamond-point paneled armoire was made in the Province of Quebec during the 18th century. Note symmetrical detailing of Louis XIII decorative paneling. (*Courtesy, Montreal Museum of Fine Arts*)

Birch desk, of Louis XIV design, originated in Canada during the 18th century. Exaggerated cabriole legs and crudely blocked drawer front mark this as the work of a rural craftsman. (*Courtesy, National Gallery of Canada*)

Profusion of scrolls and shells that appear on this small pine armoire is characteristic of ornate carved decorations found on Quebec armoires and commodes of the late 18th century. (*Courtesy, National Museum of Man*)

Provincial pine commode, made in the Louis XV manner, was built in Quebec during the 18th century. Undulating shape of front closely resembles similar work done in France. (*Courtesy, Musée du Quebec*)

50

While, to the present day, the Province of Quebec in Canada remains very French in language and customs, we seem to have lost sight of the fact that the French once occupied vast areas of our present United States. French names of places still apply, from Belle Isle twelve hundred miles westward to Duluth — and then southward along the Mississippi River to Baton Rouge and New Orleans.

While Canada was first settled as a vast fur-trading territory, the occupations of Canadian settlers eventually gave way to other pursuits. Agriculture and the lumber trade soon became the major colonial industries.

In the late seventeenth century, Frenchmen born in Canada were already identifying themselves separately as Canadians. There were two classes of Canadian society: (1) the *seigneurs* — civil officials, military officers and wealthy merchants; and (2) the farmers, minor merchants, tradesmen, craftsmen and laborers. The latter group formed the majority and were known as *habitants*.

The upper class lived in Canada in much the same way as the *bourgeoisie* lived in France. They dressed in the fashions of France and furnished their homes in the styles of the old country.

French Canadian Furniture

French pioneers, who first came to Canada during the early seventeenth century, brought very little furniture with them. Perhaps a sea chest containing their clothes and essential pieces of equipment would be all there was room for in the crowded holds of the small ships which brought them over. Faced with the vital concerns of surviving in a severe and hostile environment, the early colonists constructed their own crude furniture, mostly utility pieces hewn from rough-cut planks.

By 1650, however, skilled craftsmen had arrived in the colonies and set up shops in towns and cities along the St. Lawrence Valley. Here, they produced furniture resembling that made in France. The abundance of wood which the New World provided facilitated their task. However, hardwoods fashionable in France were not too

Serpentine-fronted commode, of 18th century Quebec origin, displays fine proportions and details of design. Note ornate hardware. This piece is characteristic of some of the finer interpretations in Canada of Louis XV design. (*Courtesy, National Gallery of Canada*)

Diamond-point paneled chest, of 18th century origin, is decorated in typical Louis XIII manner. (*Photographed by author at Montreal Museum of Fine Arts*) See measured drawing, page 190.

Provincial chest (*coffre*) with curved feet, of late 18th century origin, is a rare Canadian example of almost total lack of decorative treatment. (*Courtesy, Musée du Quebec*)

easily found in Canada. So the craftsman soon adapted himself to the use of native soft woods. After 1700, pine became a favorite for furniture making. Walnut and butternut were often used for heavier pieces. And birch, maple, basswood, cherry and elm were also frequently used.

The article of furniture most frequently found in the homes of early French Canadian settlers was the simple joined chest. Constructed usually of pine planks, often mortised and tenoned and pegged together, the chest could either be flat-topped (*coffre*) or dome-topped (*bahut*). These chests, as shown on pages 46, 51 and 52, varied in design. Some had geometrical front panels, while others had curved panels and cabriole feet. Many were painted and decorated with floral or bird motifs.

During the early eighteenth century the chest was replaced or supplemented by a large storage piece called an *armoire*. These massive pieces were inspired by the Renaissance and Louis XIII designs of France. As shown on these pages, they consisted of paneled doors framed by heavy moldings and carved with geometric designs — most notably of *diamond-point* patterns.

Other French Canadian armoires, shown on pages 49, 50 and 55, were of the more sophis-

ticated Louis XV design. These had elaborately scrolled panels and cabriole feet.

A quaint variety of benches, stools and simple chairs originated throughout the Canadian provinces. Seats of joined chairs were woven of elm, ash or rush. The legs were either squared or turned in distinctive patterns. Many of the French Canadian chairs had their direct counterparts in products of the provinces of France. But others may be distinguished by mixtures of stylistic influences and sturdy lines, which mark them as being typically "French Canadian."

Of course, for the wealthier colonists a variety of Renaissance forms were available, including sophisticated side chairs and armchairs with turned legs and rails made in the manner of Louis XIII. Classical turned chairs, as well as other more refined types, were made by Canadian craftsmen who copied the lines of imported French prototypes. They continued to be made in Canada long after their popularity had ceased in France.

Aside from the usual items of chests, chairs, commodes, armoires, tables and beds, the French Canadian craftsmen also made an unusual assortment of utility items. These included large food larders (*garde mangers*), dough boxes (*huches*),

Lidded chests of simple construction served as general storage pieces throughout the 17th and much of the 18th century. This 18th century example is fitted with a tray to hold sweet-scented herbs. (*Courtesy, National Museum of Man*)

Joint stools, with legs turned in the manner of Louis XIII, were frequently used in French Canadian churches, monasteries and homes of the 17th and 18th centuries. (*Courtesy, Musée du Quebec*)

Pine *banc-lit*, or fold-out bench-bed, is painted to simulate "grained" pattern. It is decorated with yellow liner and gilt stencil. From ballroom, Upper Canada Village, near Morrisburg, Ontario. (*Courtesy, Upper Canada Village*)

Two-tiered 18th century glazed buffet has bracket feet, suggests English influence. (*Photographed by author at Montreal Museum of Fine Arts*)

Glazed corner cabinet is made in two tiers with beveled sides. The doors have scrolled upper rails. Vertical and horizontal panels decorate the stiles and lower door. This is an 18th century cabinet of French derivation. (*Courtesy, Musée du Quebec*)

sideboards (*dressoires*) and other items. Some of the sideboards were built integrally into early Quebec houses which have since been destroyed.

The Louis XIII style remained popular in Quebec until the end of the eighteenth century. But by 1750, the more flamboyant lines of the Régence and Louis XV styles started to penetrate into the provinces. Near the end of the century the earlier rectilinear shapes and turned under-structures were replaced by the more pleasing curves and elaborate decorations of the Louis XV style.

Near the end of the eighteenth century, English furniture styles began to appear at Quebec and Montreal. English and Scottish woodworkers and cabinetmakers introduced the designs of Queen Anne, Chippendale, Adam and Sheraton. Finer woods, such as mahogany, rosewood and walnut, were used.

In 1787, English chair makers in Montreal and Quebec started to make chairs and armchairs in the English Windsor style — which they painted pale green. Of course, the new furniture of English style was not too popular in rural regions, but it did influence urban cabinetmakers. Even the traditional commodes, armoires, chests and tables took on an English look, while retaining some French characteristics.

American influences of furniture design filtered into Canada from New England. Some low buffets and commodes were copied from designs which originated in the States. Canopied and hooded cradles, made by the Mennonites of Pennsylvania, found their way into Canada. Chair-tables, or hutch-tables, of New England or Pennsylvania origin were duplicated by Canadian craftsmen. Even the American Hitchcock chair, which became so popular after 1830, was widely copied in French Canada.

But, by and large, French Canadian furniture is a style apart. It is best recognized in the designs of the seventeenth and eighteenth centuries. Thereafter there emerged an amalgam of various design influences — some European, some American. However, the end product usually represented itself as something separately "French Canadian," as identified by the antiques shown in this chapter and elsewhere.

Intricately carved and decorated 18th century armoire dominates this corner of the Maison du Calvet in Montreal. This shows the progress of the armoire, influenced by Louis XV design, from earlier diamond-point paneled models. Otherwise, this authentic French Canadian room displays a settle-bed and early side table. (*Courtesy, Montreal Museum of Fine Arts*)

Shaker slat-back rocker with rung instead of finials atop the back posts. The rung was used to attach "upholstery mats." Pedestal sewing table with two-way drawers was designed to accommodate two Shaker sisters working together. Both pieces were made at Hancock, Massachusetts, around the middle of the 19th century. (*Courtesy, Index of American Design*) See measured drawing of sewing table, page 161.

American Shaker

One hundred and fifty-four years after the Pilgrims arrived at Plymouth, another English religious faction, the *Shakers,* also immigrated to America. The Shakers, who were formally known as *"The United Society of Believers in Christ's Second Appearing,"* were persecuted in England because of their unorthodox beliefs and unique religious rituals.

Fundamentally, the Shakers believed the Second Coming of Christ was close at hand. To prepare for this, they sought to purify their souls by engaging in communal life, which involved confession of sins, community of goods, celibacy and withdrawal from the sinful world. Their way of worship called for eccentric practices to demonstrate their devotion to God. They engaged in dances, during which they literally *shook* to express their jubilation — and, to cast off evil, when they joined in emotional outbursts of prayer for salvation.

But despite the eccentricities of their religious rituals, the Shakers were essentially a God-fearing and highly industrious cult. Led from England by their "Prophetess," Mother Ann Lee, nine of them arrived in New York on August 6, 1774. Soon thereafter they established their first American commune at Niskeyuna (now Watervliet, New York), about eight miles northwest of Albany.

Despite American persecutions, which sometimes exceeded those experienced in England, the Shakers were able to convert others to their faith. Moving east from their original commune at Niskeyuna, they first organized communities at New Lebanon, New York, and then Hancock, Massachusetts. Continuing their proselytizing missions with the help of American converts, they then went on to establish Shaker communes at Enfield, Connecticut; Canterbury and Enfield, New Hampshire; Tyringham, Harvard and Shirley, Massachusetts; and Alfred and New Gloucester, Maine. Ultimately, they moved west to establish communes in Ohio, Kentucky and Indiana.

The key to the success of Shaker communal life was their dedication to the pursuit of hard work. Their leader, Mother Ann Lee, had enjoined them to put their "hands to work and hearts to God." Apparently they followed Mother Ann's admonition with diligence and skill. For wherever their communes took root, they immediately engaged in extraordinary enterprise to make them grow and prosper.

Living in isolated rural communities, they depended on agriculture as their main means of living. But soon their skill at diversified shopwork came to the fore. Because of their advanced production techniques all of their enterprises thrived. This was true, particularly, of their furniture-making industry, which, from the start, represented a distinct departure from conventional designs and methods to create a uniquely functional Shaker style.

Shaker sewing table is believed to have been built at Hancock, Massachusetts, around the middle of the 19th century. The dropleaf at the back was extended for cutting and laying out work. (*Photographed by author at the Shaker Museum, Old Chatham, New York*) See measured drawing, page 154.

Shaker Furniture

Of their many industries, inventions and communal endeavors, the Shakers have come to be best known for their fine furniture. As early as 1789, Shaker craftsmen started building furniture at New Lebanon, New York. In this community, as in all others, membership was made up in part of skilled artisans. Many of them had worked as furniture makers before they joined the Shakers.

Shaker furniture is, above all, *functional*. It works and it serves. In strict adherence to practical principles, it discards all adornment or decorative embellishment which does not contribute to functional requirements. Whatever beauty it

attains — and most Shaker designs are beautiful — is not produced by deliberately striving for beauty. Rather, it is a by-product of the Shakers' dedication to fine craftsmanship in endeavoring to create something perfect unto its purpose.

Shaker craftsmen followed the traditional solid-wood designs of early America. But restrictions of the Shaker religion applied to their work as well as their worship. Thus, they were enjoined by their Elders to strictly avoid all pretense or superfluity in the performance of their work. So, Shaker craftsmen departed from the practices of earlier colonial craftsmen by designing their furniture without elaborate scrollwork or ornamental turning. Such embellishment they regarded as "worldly show." Instead, they made their furniture perfectly plain.

Most impressive was the discipline of Shaker workmanship — its economy of structure that produced strength even when all parts were lightly and delicately made.

During the decades following their start at New Lebanon, furniture making — particularly the making of chairs — became an important element of Shaker industry. Recognizing the superiority of Shaker products, people at that time were eager to buy Shaker furniture.

The native woods used to make Shaker furniture differed in various localities. While in New York and New England pine, birch, oak, maple, cherry, hickory and butternut were commonly used, in the western states walnut, cherry, beech and poplar seemed to be more abundantly available. By and large, however, the edicts of the Central Ministry at New Lebanon were followed in all areas — and in many instances it is difficult to determine the regional origins of Shaker designs.

This handsome turned trestle table was built by the Shakers of Hancock, Massachusetts, before 1840. The low-back dining chairs were made at Watervliet, New York, around 1830. (*Photographed by author at the Shaker Museum, Old Chatham, New York*) See measured drawings of similar trestle table and dining chairs, pages 153 and 138.

Curly maple side chair was made by the Harvard Shakers around 1850. (*Photographed by author at Fruitlands Museums*) See measured drawing, page 139.

This low-back rush-seated dining chair was built at Hancock, Massachusetts, around 1830. (*Courtesy, Henry Ford Museum*) See measured drawing, page 138.

Unusual Shaker armchair with partially braided back is believed to have been made at New Lebanon, New York, late in the 19th century. (*Photographed by author at the Shaker Museum, Old Chatham, New York*)

Shaker Chairs and Rockers

Of the many types of furniture they produced, the Shakers were most prolific in their manufacture of chairs and rockers. Chair makers of the New Lebanon community started building their own distinctive designs, some for sale to outside markets, during the 1790s — and their business continued well into the twentieth century.

Shaker chairs gave positive expression to the religious craftsman's aspiration to produce something perfect unto its purpose. Unlike most other chairs made during their era, they were light and strong and adroitly adapted to support the human body in a comfortable seated position. While they were made in many types and sizes — from the smallest children's chairs to the tall ladder-back classics — they all possessed the virtues of being superbly crafted and beautifully suited to requirements.

The chairs best known and most widely sold by the Shakers were the so-called *ladder-backs,* which were made with bent back slats and delicately turned legs with round or pointed finials. In contrast to the tall ladder-back was the Shaker's low-back dining chair of similar construction. This was made with one or two curved slats, with the back posts shortened so that it could be tucked under the table after mealtime.

Most Shaker chairs and rockers had caned or woven seats. At first they were woven with narrow hickory splints. But after 1830, cane, rush,

This earlier design of Shaker slat-back rocker was made at New Lebanon, New York, around 1850. (*Courtesy, Henry Ford Museum*)

colorful worsted tapes and other materials were used. Near the middle of the century the Shakers invented their tilting-chair device, which was inserted under the tips of the back legs to prevent slipping or marring of floors when the chair was tilted back against a wall.

While they cannot be credited with "inventing" the rocking chair, the Shakers did more to develop its design and promote its use than any other chair makers. At first they were rather slim and severe in appearance. But after 1830, modifications in size and structure caused them to be regarded as exceptionally comfortable seating designs.

The comfort of Shaker rockers did not happen by accident. Every component of their structure was carefully measured and fitted to suit the human body. Shaker craftsmen in their search for functional perfection experimented with proportions in relation to physical requirements until they hit upon exactly the right dimensions of parts.

Shaker rockers were designed with or without arms. The most popular models had scrolled arms with "mushroom" post turnings to top off protrusions of front-leg tenons. They were made in graduated sizes, starting with diminutive children's rockers (little gems of craftsmanship) and ranging up to the "great" rockers of full adult size.

Early Shaker rocker was slim, trim and severe. This one was made around 1830. (*Courtesy, New York State Museum*)

Armless rockers were made in many Shaker communities. This example is of late 19th century origin. (*Courtesy, Index of American Design*)

Combined showing of Shaker rocker and pedestal table represents separation of time periods. The table was made around 1830, and the rocker was produced some fifty years later. (*Courtesy, Index of American Design*) See measured drawing of pedestal table, page 159.

Spindle-back Shaker rocker, with woven tape seat, is believed to have been made at New Lebanon, New York, late in the 19th century. (*Author's collection*)

Utility desk-cupboard, of pumpkin pine, was built at Hancock, Massachusetts, around 1830. It was probably used for keeping kitchen accounts. Note herbs and accessories hanging from overhead pegboard. (*Photographed by author at Hancock, Massachusetts*)

Shaker Inventiveness

The Shakers were regarded as the leading inventors of their time — and this was reflected in the design of their furniture as well as other things. Aside from their uniquely designed chairs and rockers, they created a variety of desks, chests, tables and other items designed exclusively for the requirements of individuals or to facilitate the performance of communal chores.

Most notable among these were their built-in structures containing batteries of drawers and cupboards. Also, tables were especially designed to facilitate the combined work of two or more people. On the tidy side, all interior walls had pegged strips attached for hanging things out of the way when not in use.

Desks were designed to facilitate sewing, as well as keeping communal records. Some, like the one shown on the opposite page, were especially designed to keep kitchen accounts.

Frequently, Shaker furniture was custom-made to fit the requirements of individuals. For this reason, when reviewing the types of Shaker furniture, it will be found that many unique designs appear among the assortment.

Shaker improved stove dominates the sparse furnishing of this typical dormitory. Wood box, drop-leaf table, rocker and candlestand are all early products of New York and New England Shaker communities. Side chair hangs from pegboard in usual Shaker fashion. (*Courtesy, American Museum in Britain*) See measured drawing of candlestand, page 158.

Early Shaker desk was made at Sabbathday Lake, Maine, around 1820. "Revolver chair," in front of desk, has bent metal rods supporting the back. (*Photographed by author at the Shaker Museum, Sabbathday Lake, Maine*) See measured drawing of similar revolver chair, page 142.

Shaker Chests

Living together in communal dwellings, the Shakers needed more case furniture than the average householder. Order and neatness were religious principles, in the practice of which the Shakers provided "a place for everything and everthing in its place." They did this by building ample storage facilities. Everything that was not in actual use was immediately put away in drawers and cupboards to avoid even the slightest hint of clutter or untidiness.

Lidded blanket chests, which graduated into lidded chests with one, two or three drawers, were especially constructed for the storage of woolens and linens. Full chests of drawers, of ample capacity, were used for the storage of clothing and personal belongings.

Shaker chests of drawers were designed for beauty as well as utility. Most of them were superbly proportioned with the drawer widths graduated — narrow at the top and wide at the bottom — to produce harmonious effects of lightness and fine balance. Taller chests, which required steps for access to the top drawers, and massive chest-cupboards were shared by several members of the community. Apparently, separate drawers were assigned to each individual.

Sometimes the design of western Shaker chests of drawers became a bit "worldly" in the use of scrolled aprons and other mild forms of surface embellishment. One western chest, which was autographed by the craftsman, indicating that it was built at Union Village, Ohio, in 1827, bears a remarkably close resemblance to a French Provincial design of the same era. More frequently, however, the western Shaker chests — particularly those built in southern Kentucky — are heavier and more ponderous than those made in the eastern communities.

Combinations of chests of drawers with top cupboards were used for general storage in working areas of the Shaker dwellings, as well as in the dormitories. Obviously, the assorted *sets of steps*, which the Shakers also designed, were needed to climb up to the top cupboards.

Large and small drawerless wall cupboards — beautifully built, with dovetailed corners and through-tenoned and pegged door frames — were made for various uses. These were attached to walls of kitchens and workrooms to store the tools and utensils of domestic pursuits.

This pine sewing desk is believed to have been made by the Shakers at New Lebanon, New York, around 1850. (*Courtesy, Henry Ford Museum*)

Earliest form of Shaker blanket chest was built around 1820. Made of pumpkin pine, this example is nicely proportioned and carefully dovetailed at all corners. (*Courtesy, the Shaker Museum, Old Chatham, New York*)

Pine lidded chest, with one drawer, was made at an eastern Shaker community around the middle of the 19th century. With addition of bottom drawers, the box-type chest ultimately evolved into a full chest of drawers. (*Courtesy, Henry Ford Museum*)

This handsome lidded chest, with two drawers, was built by the Shakers at New Lebanon, New York, around 1820. (*Photographed by author at the Shaker Museum, Old Chatham, New York*) See measured drawing, page 194.

Here's what happened when the Shakers discarded their lidded chest tops and started to make full chests of drawers. This handsome pine chest was built at Harvard, Massachusetts, by Elder Joseph Myrick in 1844. (*Photographed by author at Fruitlands Museums*) See measured drawing, page 195.

This sprightly cherry table was made by the Shakers at Canterbury, New Hampshire, early in the 19th century. (*Courtesy, Henry Ford Museum*)

Shaker table made of cherry, with delicately tapered legs, was built for Sister Mary Settle of Pleasant Hill, Kentucky. (*Courtesy, Index of American Design*)

Shaker Tables

Although Shaker tables were sometimes sold outside the communities, for the most part they were designed for use by the Shakers themselves. Thus there was very little standardization of types and sizes, as would be required if they were produced in quantity. Instead, they were made in an assortment of sizes and styles, with many designs apparently custom-built for a particular purpose.

Large tables of the trestle type, designed for communal dining, were made in many models. Shaker trestle tables differed in construction from those of early American design. Those made in this country before the Shakers arrived were heavily built, with a center rail spanning midway down the leg posts. Shaker craftsmen eliminated the excessive weight and connected their center rails up underneath the top where they would not obstruct the legs and knees of those seated at the table.

Shaker trestle tables measured up to twenty feet in length — although the usual top dimensions were approximately ten feet by three feet. Shorter models were made for the two Elders and the two Eldresses, who sat together at mealtimes. The earliest trestles were plainly built, with chamfered posts and flat, tapered feet. Later the feet were arched (probably to allow toe room at the ends), and the posts were either scroll-shaped or turned.

Although pine was most frequently used for the tops, a variety of other woods, including ash, oak, maple, cherry and walnut, were used for other parts. Some of the ministry tables were made entirely of cherry or walnut. Walnut was most frequently used in the western Shaker communities.

Among other tables of Shaker design, the assortment seems almost limitless. Tables came in all shapes and sizes, ranging from the little bedside stands with delicately turned legs to the huge types already described.

Following their practice of eliminating all excess weight, the light tables (which the Shakers sometimes called "nice") were precisely proportioned, with all parts shaved down to minimum thickness.

Many Shaker tables were designed to facilitate certain types of work. Sometimes the apron drawers were staggered on both sides and ends so that two or more members could work together around a single table. Others were more massively built for use as kitchen utility tables or for shop chores.

Apart from the trestle types and four-legged designs, the Shakers also specialized in the construction of single-standard pedestal tables. These, too, displayed exceptional individuality of style, and their assortment of sizes and types places them in a category of their own.

The "working" pedestals — or *tripod stands,* as they were sometimes called — were made with plain chamfered standards and pegged legs. Others had simple bulb-turned standards, which were angle-bored near the bottom to receive turned peglegs.

At the opposite extreme of sophisticated design were the beautifully styled Shaker pedestals with exquisitely turned stems and curved or undulating legs. These were made in the eastern colonies throughout the nineteenth century. In their free-flowing symmetry of shapes and proportions, some Shaker pedestals may be regarded as artistic masterpieces (see pages 158–159).

Western Shaker cherry bed, with trundle bed below, was built at Union Village, Ohio, around 1830. Note Shaker candle sconce and tree-of-life spirit drawing hanging on wall. (*Photographed by author at the Warren County Historical Museum*)

Shakers' round and oval boxes and carriers were made in graduated sizes of assorted types. (*Courtesy, New York State Museum*)

Flawless craftsmanship of Shaker oval boxes is evident in this specimen made of birch and pine. (*Courtesy, Henry Ford Museum*)

A skilled Hitchcock artist, working with quills just as of old, gold-stripes a Hitchcock chair. Favorite decorative stencils appear on the back chair panel and rung. For today's production, several artists apply stencils and gold striping to approximately one hundred chairs a day. (*Courtesy, The Hitchcock Chair Co.*)

Other Regional Influences

From the eighteenth to the twentieth century, pockets of exceptionally noteworthy furniture designs originated throughout this country. Some of these influences were widely heralded, like the design of the celebrated Hitchcock Chair. Others came from religious sects, notably the distinctive craftsmanship of the Shakers, Mennonites, Mormons, Moravians, Zoarites and other religious oriented craftsmen. Still other designs made their appearance because of the creative initiative of gifted individual craftsmen, as exemplified by the exquisitely carved furniture made by Mark Fenderson of Maine.

All such furniture is identified by its individuality of style. Of course, the predominating influences of the time prevailed. But this furniture was *different* in the sense that it asserted new ways of making common objects. Moreover, it revealed the traditional ethnic background of the maker — most often, a reflection of his European background.

Many of these pieces were made to order, using patterns and designs from the old country with which the craftsman was familiar. Some were crudely copied from pieces brought to America from across the sea. Still other pieces, of simple and unadorned character, were made by itinerant joiners for the kitchens and service rooms of wealthy colonists.

During the nineteenth century, with the growth of substantial communities and increased prosperity, came a demand for finer and more sophisticated furniture. Thus evolved the more elaborate designs of "Texas German," which seemed to represent a German version of the Victorian style. For the most part this furniture was massively built — usually by rural craftsmen.

The Scandinavians also contributed much to the design of American country furniture. While they settled most abundantly in the midwestern states of Minnesota and Wisconsin, they also immigrated to practically every other part of the country, bringing with them their native skills.

As shown on pages 77 and 78, the Norwegians, in particular, contributed much to enhance the gaiety and cheerfulness of their frontier homes with their native folk art. Their carved designs were rich with painted decorations — and made with superb skill. Their furniture undoubtedly offered a bright note of relief in contrast to its austere surroundings.

So, starting with Lambert Hitchcock's famous chairs, we may go on to consider a few other influences in the emergence of American country furniture. Of course, this only highlights the myriads of types and nationalities of distinctive designs which originated in all parts of the country. But the influences shown here seem important enough to merit separate consideration.

A popular stencil design for Hitchcock chairs. Finely ground bronze powders in golden colors are used for this artwork. (*Courtesy, The Hitchcock Chair Co.*)

Connecticut Hitchcock

Early in the nineteenth century, Lambert Hitchcock, an enterprising Connecticut Yankee, began manufacturing chair parts in his shop at Barkhamsted, Connecticut. He shipped these components in large quantities to Charleston, South Carolina. Soon, however, he started to make completely assembled chairs, which he advertised in the *Connecticut Courant* in 1822.

At the start, Hitchcock chairs were undecorated and plainly made. But young Hitchcock aspired to make something better. In fact, it was his ambition to make the best chairs in America.

Inspired by the decorative painting of early Connecticut chests and other furniture, Hitchcock decided that his chairs should be painted and elaborately decorated with stenciled designs. As an alternative to carving, inlays and mounted adornments, which made European chairs so desirable and expensive, Hitchcock chose stenciling as the most practical decorative technique within economic reach.

Thus, at his new brick factory, located at Hitchcock-ville, Connecticut (now Riverton, Connecticut), Hitchcock produced a line of decorative chairs and rockers which were shipped out and eagerly bought in cities and towns throughout America.

Indeed, popular demand for Hitchcock chairs became so great that their manufacture soon

Black button-back, crown-top Hitchcock chair was first made between 1825 and 1832. (*Courtesy, The Hitchcock Chair Co.*)

Another popular early design of Hitchcock chair employed ring turning and rush seat. (*Courtesy, Index of American Design*)

This handsome cane-seated Hitchcock chair was made between 1832 and 1840. Note application of stencil design, shown above. (*Courtesy, Index of American Design*)

reached the impressive total of over fifteen thousand chairs per year. Even this amount of production could have been exceeded if skilled artisans were available to perform the specialized manufacturing techniques. While the roster of Hitchcock employees soon exceeded one hundred, the unique artistry of hand operations involved in decorative stenciling required the services of specially trained artists.

Soon the designation "Hitchcock Chairs" became a hallmark of quality and distinction throughout America — and these chairs were widely copied both here and abroad.

After the death of Lambert Hitchcock on April 3, 1852, the chair business was discontinued. But fortunately, cessation of manufacture was only temporary. For on October 17, 1946, The Hitchcock Chair Company again came into being at Riverton, Connecticut. So today, following the patterns of more than a century ago, Hitchcock chairs are again being made — and their present popularity may now exceed that enjoyed during their original production.

This comfortable Hitchcock armchair was made to match the side chair shown at left bottom corner of opposite page. (*Courtesy, The Hitchcock Chair Co.*)

A different type of crown-top Hitchcock rocking chair was made between 1832 and 1843. This is a more advanced model, decorated with a stenciled flower basket on the crest and a floral design on front edge of the seat. (*Courtesy, The Hitchcock Chair Co.*)

Black crown-top, Salem-type rocker, with plank seat, was made between 1825 and 1832. It is signed "L. Hitchcock, Hitchcock-ville, Conn." (*Courtesy, The Hitchcock Chair Co.*)

Built around 1750 in the Shenandoah Valley of Virginia, this handsome dish dresser reflects the simplicity of rural Piedmont design. (*Courtesy, Winterthur Museum*)

Southern Plantation

Mixed as it was by Spanish, English, French and other European influences, architecture and furniture design of the pre–Civil War South represented a conglomerate of styles. Of course, the elegant interiors of affluent southern plantations contained furniture of the most stylish sort — including the mahogany pieces of Chippendale, Sheraton, Hepplewhite and the Adam brothers. Some of this was imported from abroad — although much was made by urban cabinetmakers of New York, Philadelphia, Charleston and other cities where advanced techniques of fine furniture construction had been mastered.

But, by way of "country furniture" made in rural regions of the South, there emerged many noteworthy designs. These pieces were made by country craftsmen and generally followed, in a less sophisticated way, the designs originating in urban centers. Ordinarily, they were built of solid wood and lacked ornate details of carving, inlays and other adornments found on their city-made counterparts.

Much of the southern plantation furniture was constructed by carpenters and joiners who were part of the personnel of particular plantations. Thus, many of these pieces were made by slaves who had served their apprenticeship under skilled craftsmen.

An especially interesting example of slave-made plantation furniture is shown below. This

This distinguished walnut gate-leg table was built by slaves for statesman Patrick Henry in the late 18th century. Its delicate treatment of apron scrolls and Dutch-footed cabriole legs combines with its perfect proportions to make this an unusually fine example of early craftsmanship. (*Courtesy, Index of American Design*)

This rugged rocker, with five shaped slats and button-topped finials, was made on a plantation in Merriwether County, Georgia, early in the 19th century. (*Courtesy, Atlanta Historical Society*)

Georgia-pine plantation desk is assembled in two parts, with paneled doors and compartmented top cupboard resting atop the taper-legged lower desk. This piece was built in rural Georgia early in the 19th century. (*Courtesy, Atlanta Historical Society*)

Pine blanket chest was built on a plantation at Clarke County, Alabama, around 1830. (*Courtesy, Carlen House Museum*)

Made of pine with buttermilk and red-clay finish, this pie safe has tin sides and door panels, which are perforated with tree-of-life and other circular patterns. It is believed to have been made on a plantation in Tennessee during the 19th century. (*Courtesy, Atlanta Historical Society*)

handsome walnut gate-leg table is believed to have been made by slaves in Virginia for Patrick Henry. Details of this delicate Dutch-foot design combine to make it a model of fine proportions and symmetry of line. While of rural origin, it ranks with the most advanced furniture designs of its era.

Some plantation furniture, notably the desk shown above at right, was especially designed to serve a specific purpose. This desk, apparently, was made to assist the plantation owner with the chores of keeping household or business accounts. Shelves and compartments at the top could be used for filing bills and documents, while there was ample room beneath the lidded counter for storing heavy reference materials.

The slat-back rocking chair shown above reveals the curious resemblance of rocker designs originating in various parts of the country. While this example was made at Merriwether County, Georgia, early in the 19th century, it comes close to Shaker design and also resembles similar rockers made in many other places throughout the country.

Carved oak wall cupboard, built by Mark Fenderson of Farmington, Maine, late in the 19th century, shows carefully dovetailed construction and uniquely carved designs. Note staggered door pulls, which blend into carving of door stiles. (*Courtesy, Maine State Museum*)

Detailed view of front of Fenderson wall cupboard shows exquisite carving of woodland scene. As an artist, Fenderson was able to transfer his creative designs to wood, giving them the full depth and shadow of three-dimensional wood sculpture. (*Courtesy, Maine State Museum*)

Maine Curiosities

The state of Maine abounds with antique furniture designs influenced by the mixed nationalities of its early settlers. Conspicuous among these were the works of English, French, Dutch, German and Scandinavian craftsmen — all of whom were represented among the colonists. Thus much of the furniture of Maine falls into the conglomerate category called "Early American."

But here and there some distinctive designs appeared which could be credited to the creative acumen of individuals rather than representing mass expression.

For instance, the delicate little desk boxes at right, made by the Meservey Cabinet Works of Bangor, Maine, around 1850, show superlative skill and an unusual degree of individuality. These are made of extremely thin walnut boards, intricately joined and assembled for precise fitting of hinged lids and compartmented bodies. They are so exquisitely crafted that the thought of their being mass-produced would seem to be impossible. Still, they were the products of an industrial cabinet company, which would indicate that they were commercially made and merchandised.

But for perfection of artistic detail in the making of carved furniture, it would be difficult to surpass the work of Mark Fenderson — shown right and on the facing page. Oddly enough, Fenderson spent his boyhood at Farmington, Maine, where at an early age he demonstrated exceptional talent as an artist and cartoonist. In later years he gained national fame as a cartoonist, contributing to such magazines as the old *Life*.

But his first love was woodcarving. He used wood as *paper* and carving tools as a *pencil* to literally illustrate in wood. He had uncanny ability at handling perspective to achieve by line, light and shadow effects of distance and space not commonly found in woodcarving. The furniture he made was styled according to his own design and then elaborately carved in his own inimitable fashion.

Fenderson's work, as illustrated here, represented a form of wood sculpture which, while originating in Maine during the early twentieth century, resembles ecclesiastical carving of medieval times.

This delicately constructed desk box was made by the Meservey Cabinet Company of Bangor, Maine, around 1850. All parts are made of thin sheets of walnut, intricately joined at the corners and assembled with slim hinges. A velvet panel covers the writing surfaces. (*Courtesy, Maine State Museum*) See measured drawing, page 185.

Mark Fenderson's rendition of a carved Bible box depicts biblical scenes on five surfaces. This was another of the allegorical carving motifs which Fenderson applied so effectively to his work. (*Courtesy, Maine State Museum*)

Ohio Zoar

Around 1817, a small German sect known as the Zoarites immigrated to Ohio. Like other religious groups, they came to this country so that they could continue to practice their religion unmolested and free of persecution. Their religious faith advocated some strange practices, including the wearing of unconventional apparel, strict vegetarianism, refusal to yield to some civic laws and, for a while, celibacy.

Approximately three hundred Zoarites first arrived in Ohio to farm and build a town. At first they were so energetically occupied that celibacy was adopted to free the women of childbearing, which would interfere with their farm work. By 1830, however, when their farms had been established and their town built, celibacy was discontinued.

Contrary to the strictness of Zoar discipline, their furniture was brightly made with decorative elements typical of native German work. Chests, hanging cupboards and beds bore the imprint of Zoar craftsmanship. Usually such items were painted gray-blue, with colorful decorative motifs applied to relieve plain surfaces. Later, Zoar furniture followed the Sheraton and Empire styles, but it was made more ponderously — and with plenty of painted decorations.

The Ohio Zoar community was disbanded in 1898, and their furniture was distributed among surviving members. Very little remains, except for those pieces which can still be seen at the museum in Zoar, Ohio.

"Blue Bonnet Cabinet" of black walnut, painted blue and adorned with flowers and birds, was made by craftsmen of the Zoar, Ohio, community in 1836. (*Courtesy, Index of American Design*)

Traditional German plank chair, made by Zoar craftsmen late in the 19th century, has oak legs and pine seat and back. (*Courtesy, Henry Ford Museum*)

Child's bed was made at a Zoar, Ohio, cabinet shop early in the 19th century. Note ingenious use of removable guardrails. (*Courtesy, Index of American Design*)

Norwegian American

Highly decorative furniture was both imported and built at the many Scandinavian settlements throughout the country. Particularly in the states of Minnesota and Wisconsin, Swedes, Norwegians and Danes brought their native cultures to the new land, where they perpetuated the craft industries of the old country. Most of their work is impressive for its blending of carving and flamboyant painted decorations into furniture that is both attractive and practical.

Uniquely distinctive is the work of Wisconsin pioneers. Here, entire communities settled in surroundings bearing a striking resemblance in topography and climate to their native Norway. They built their log farmhouses in the valleys and then furnished and decorated them in the same fashion as their birthplaces across the seas.

The buildings they erected followed traditional Norwegian architectural designs. Sod roofs were common over log structures. Many were built with roof cupolas and painted a warm, fresh blue. Some had dragon heads carved at the peaks of the gables and shingles shaped to resemble fish scales. All were picturesque.

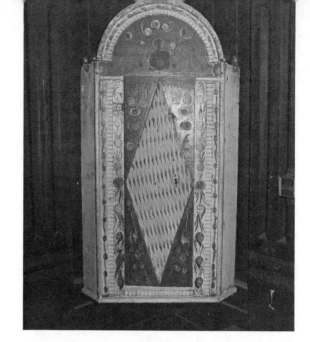

Elaborately decorated Norwegian corner cupboard, or *skop*, has date carved on top indicating that it was built in 1859. Entire front of cupboard is decoratively painted with Norwegian rosemaling. (*Courtesy, Little Norway Museum*)

Sturdy Norwegian chest, liberally decorated with rosemaling, was built in 1756. It was originally used by immigrants to bring their belongings to America. (*Courtesy, Little Norway Museum*)

Folding wall table, known by the Norwegian name *klappbord*, was a standard fixture in many early Norwegian homes. This example was made by Paul E. Bjerkeng, who emigrated from Tonsit, Norway, to Beldenville, Wisconsin, in 1857. (*Courtesy, Vesterheim, Norwegian-American Museum*)

Interior of Little Norway Museum displays a lively assortment of furniture and artifacts used in early Norwegian American homes. Note griffin-shaped armchair in foreground and elaborate shaping and carving of woodwork. Typical Norwegian cupboard, replete with burnished-copper utensils and dishes, was built around 1868. The entire cupboard (inside and out) is decorated with colorful Norwegian *rosemaling*. (*Courtesy, Little Norway Museum*)

Another interior view of Little Norway Museum shows assorted trunks, boxes, tubs and tankards — all of Norwegian American origin. On the back wall, an elaborately scrolled cupboard displays colorful *rosemaling* decorations. (*Courtesy, Little Norway Museum*)

Three-legged Norwegian *bandestol* has dragon-shaped arm tips and colorfully painted *rosemaling* decorations applied to all parts. These three-legged chairs not only fit conveniently into corners but also balanced themselves on uneven sod floors of early Norwegian homes. (*Courtesy, Little Norway Museum*)

Drop-leaf desk is believed to have been made by a Norwegian craftsman around 1870 at Fergus Falls, Minnesota. The accompanying tub chair, or *kubbestol*, was made around 1850 in a rural area adjoining Racine, Wisconsin. (*Courtesy, Vesterheim, Norwegian-American Museum*)

Indoors, all woodworking was either elaborately carved or turned. The use of colorful paints and contrasting painted decorations transformed the interiors into wonderlands of animated artwork. All of the mystical motifs of Norwegian lore were employed to create distinctively attractive rooms.

Included among the furniture are Norwegian open cupboards, long tables, gate-leg tables, fold-up tables, three-legged chairs, tub chairs and other pieces, all highly decorated with both carving and *rosemaling* — a unique Norwegian art of painted decoration.

Rosemaling goes somewhat beyond the Pennsylvania folk art of painted furniture decoration in its endless variety of motifs and its vividness of color. Most of the patterns employ leaves, scrolls, fruits, flowers, vegetables, birds and animals, all reproduced in the brightest colors. Many rosemaling designs date back several centuries, while others are freshly created by new practitioners of the art. Sometimes written messages or biblical quotations were inscribed in embellished lettering as part of a rosemaling composition.

As shown here, Norwegian American furniture is picturesque, practical and, in many instances, inventive. Obviously, with its bright decorations, it is also cheerful. It appears to strike a note of pleasing contrast to the sedate and sober nature of its makers.

Butternut chest of drawers was built during the 1860s at Decorah, Iowa. It came from the parsonage of the first Norwegian Lutheran minister west of the Mississippi River. (*Courtesy, Vesterheim, Norwegian-American Museum*)

Primitive Norwegian gate-leg table has leaves which extend to the floor. It was built during the 1850s at a rural area near Decorah, Iowa. (*Courtesy, Vesterheim, Norwegian-American Museum*)

Draw-leaf extension table of walnut was made in New Braunfels, Comal County, Texas, around 1870. (*Courtesy, Winedale Inn, University of Texas at Austin*)

For more than three hundred years the present state of Texas was part of the Spanish colonial empire. Since Spain insisted that her colonies engage in trade exclusively with the mother country, the early furniture of Texas was necessarily Spanish. With the independence of Mexico (including Texas) from Spain, an influx of people started to migrate to Texas from the southern states.

But the real wave of immigration started around 1830, when large numbers of Europeans — mostly German — moved to Texas. These people were seeking escape from the chaos and oppression of post-Napoleonic Germany. The rising militarism which became part of German unification also influenced their movement.

The German immigrants brought with them the styles and tastes of their native land. And in Texas they applied the skills of their trades learned through age-old systems of apprenticeship and guilds.

Walnut and cedar washstand was made at Brenham, Washington County, Texas, around 1860. (*Courtesy, Winedale Inn, University of Texas at Austin*)

Sewing table of walnut was made at Round Top, Fayette County, Texas, around 1850. Cabriole legs and delicate proportions distinguish this as one of the finer country designs of Texas origin. (*Courtesy, Winedale Inn, University of Texas at Austin*)

Pine chest of drawers, made in Navasota, Grimes County, Texas, around 1870, displays fine proportions and tasteful application of molded adornments. (*Courtesy, Winedale Inn, University of Texas at Austin*)

Handsome walnut cabinet has nice proportions and shows careful attention to details of design. It is believed to have been handmade by a rural German craftsman at Weimar, Texas, around 1870. (*Courtesy, Winedale Inn, University of Texas at Austin*)

Pine pie safe, with punched tin panels, was collected at Harris County, Texas, where it was believed to have been built by a rural craftsman around 1870. This is a beautifully built and skillfully decorated piece. (*Courtesy, Winedale Inn, University of Texas at Austin*)

Before industrialization, which did not take place in Texas until late in the nineteenth century, all furniture was handmade and often custom-built to meet individual requirements.

After Texas became an independent Republic, the number of immigrants increased substantially. New communities were started, and older settlements experienced new growth. Because of the vast distances between places, each ranch and remote community was isolated and had to become self-sufficient to meet its own requirements.

Thus, a particular locality might be favored with the services of a skilled cabinetmaker, while others had to be content with crude carpentry. But by and large, a separate style of Texas furniture emerged, which may be described as massively handsome.

Particularly interesting were the large wardrobes, or *schranks,* which were made not only to provide ample storage space but also, seemingly, to serve as status symbols in early Texas German homes. These, together with massive chests and dressers and stately tester-topped beds, some of which are pictured on these pages, tended to make Texas German furniture of the nineteenth century a style apart. Much of it, as exhibited in museums in Texas, is distinguished by its superb workmanship and careful attention to fine details of design.

Ornate high-post walnut bed, built by Johann Umland of Washington County, Texas, in 1861, displays sophistication of design and decorative detail not generally achieved by rural craftsmen. (*Courtesy, Winedale Inn, University of Texas at Austin*)

II COUNTRY CATEGORIES: COMPARISON OF REGIONAL INFLUENCES

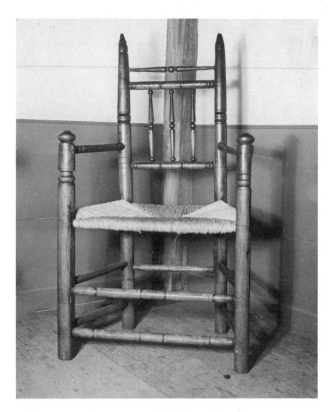

Governor Carver armchair, dated around 1650, is still in use at Longfellow's Wayside Inn. (*Courtesy, Longfellow's Wayside Inn*)

Windsor writing-armchair, made in New England during last quarter of the 18th century, shows unusual turning of arm supports. (*Courtesy, Longfellow's Wayside Inn*)

Side chair, also of Governor Carver design, displays typical turning and rush seat. (*Courtesy, Metropolitan Museum of Art*)

Cromwellian upholstered side chair was made in New England during last half of the 17th century. Leather upholstery had become popular in more affluent homes of that period. (*Courtesy, Henry Ford Museum*)

Top left. Spanish armchair of late 18th century origin was made in (or imported to) California. Note intricate carving. (*Courtesy, Index of American Design*)

Top right. French Canadian 18th century slat-back chair is beautifully proportioned and constructed. (*Courtesy, Upper Canada Village*)

Center. Canadian side chair, made on the Isle of Orleans during the 18th century, reflects influences of French Provincial style. (*Courtesy, Musée du Quebec*)

Bottom left. Hand-tooled leather, combined with carving and decorative use of large-headed upholstery tacks, distinguishes this early Spanish side chair from California. (*Courtesy, Index of American Design*)

Bottom right. Hackberry slat-back chair, with leather bottom, was made in La Grange, Texas, late in the 19th century. (*Courtesy Winedale Inn, University of Texas at Austin*)

WINDSOR CHAIRS

Assorted Windsor chairs, assembled in Commons Room of Winterthur Museum, include comb-back armchair, bow-back side chair, low-back armchairs and unusual Windsor settee. All of these Windsors originated in New England and the Middle Atlantic states during the 18th century. (*Courtesy, Winterthur Museum*)

Gracefully designed painted Windsor armchair was made by Joel Pratt, Jr., of Sterling, Massachusetts, between 1820 and 1830. (*Courtesy, Henry Ford Museum*)

Fan-back Windsor side chair with bamboo turning is believed to have been made by "S. Pugh" of Augusta, Georgia, early in the 19th century. (*Courtesy, Atlanta Historical Society*)

Plain bow-back Windsor side chair with scooped plank seat is believed to have been made in Delaware during the early 19th century. (*Courtesy, Index of American Design*)

Early comb-back Windsor writing-armchair has drawer beneath seat for holding writing materials. Other Windsors of this type also had drawers beneath the writing arm. (*Courtesy, Index of American Design*)

Bow-back Windsor armchair, made in New England between 1775 and 1800, was originally painted black. (*Courtesy, Henry Ford Museum*)

Low-back Windsor writing-armchair was originally used at Harvard College during early 19th century. (*Courtesy, Index of American Design*)

Top left. Hitchcock chair, bearing stencil "L. Hitchcock, Hitchcock-ville, Connecticut," was made between 1825 and 1828. (*Courtesy, Henry Ford Museum*)

Top right. Elaborately decorated Connecticut chair was made at East Haven early in the 19th century. (*Courtesy, Index of American Design*)

Center. Norwegian painted *bandestol* has three legs and is lavishly decorated with *rosemaling*. (*Courtesy, Little Norway Museum*)

Bottom left. Zoar plank chair, made at Zoar, Ohio, during 19th century, is of traditional German design. (*Courtesy, Henry Ford Museum*)

Bottom right. Simple, functional side chair of Scandinavian design, made by Bishop Hill, Illinois craftsmen, between 1846 and 1850. (*Courtesy, Index of American Design*)

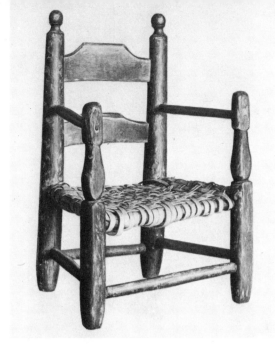

Top left. Child's chair, made by slaves on Texas plantation prior to 1860. (*Courtesy, Index of American Design*)

Top right. Shaker armchair, made at New Lebanon, New York, during later years of the 19th century. (*Photographed by author, courtesy, The Shaker Museum, Old Chatham, New York*)

Middle. Child's high chair, made in New England around 1830. (*Photographed by author, courtesy, Fruitlands Museums*)

Bottom left. Child's wing chair, made of pine, was built in North Carolina around 1790. Chair doubles as seat and commode. (*Courtesy, Atlanta Historical Society*)

Bottom right. Windsor high chair was made in New England between 1765 and 1780. (*Courtesy, Winterthur Museum*)

Top left. This crudely constructed rocker was made in a rural region of Maryland during early years of the 19th century. (*Courtesy, Index of American Design*)

Top right. Armless rocker, made in Iowa in 1837, has legs of oak, rockers of walnut, spindles of hickory and seat and back of maple. (*Courtesy, Index of American Design*)

Middle. Rhode Island rocker from mid-19th century has curved arms, saddle seat and eccentrically curved back spindles. (*Courtesy, Index of American Design*)

Bottom left. Boston stenciled rocker of early 19th century has typical crested headpiece and deeply curved seat, arms and spindles. This is an excellent example of the Boston classic. (*Courtesy, Henry Ford Museum*)

Hitchcock rocker, made in Connecticut between 1832 and 1840, is painted black and decorated with typical Hitchcock stencils. (*Courtesy, Index of American Design*)

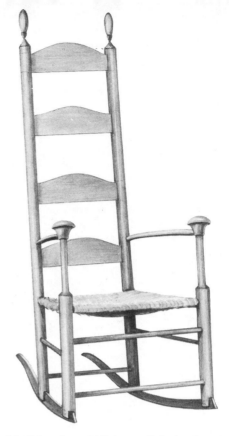

Top left. Light and graceful Shaker spindle-back rocker is believed to have been made at New Lebanon, New York, toward the end of the 19th century. (*Author's collection*)

Top right. Early Shaker rocker was made at Enfield, Connecticut, at the beginning of the 19th century. It exemplifies simplicity and severity of early Shaker design. (*Courtesy, Index of American Design*)

Middle. Rawhide-seated Texas rocker of the mid-19th century shows complete individuality in details of turning and construction. (*Courtesy, Index of American Design*)

Bottom left. Side rocker, believed to have been· made in Pennsylvania around 1820, introduces a new twist in rocking motion. (*Courtesy, Index of American Design*)

Bottom right. Shakers of New Lebanon, New York, stretched their ingenuity to invent this rocker, which both rocks and swivels. (*Courtesy, Index of American Design*)

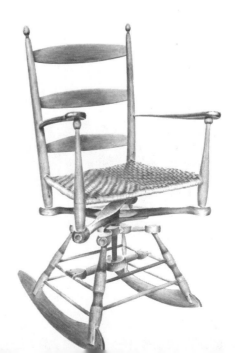

This "grandfather" of early American settles was built in New England during the 17th century. (*Courtesy, Metropolitan Museum of Art*)

Pennsylvania wagon bench was built around 1780. Seat was designed to alternate between wagon and home. (*Courtesy, Index of American Design*)

Shaker meetinghouse benches of the type illustrated were built at Canterbury, New Hampshire, early in the 19th century. This design was followed in many other Shaker communities. (*Courtesy, Henry Ford Museum*)

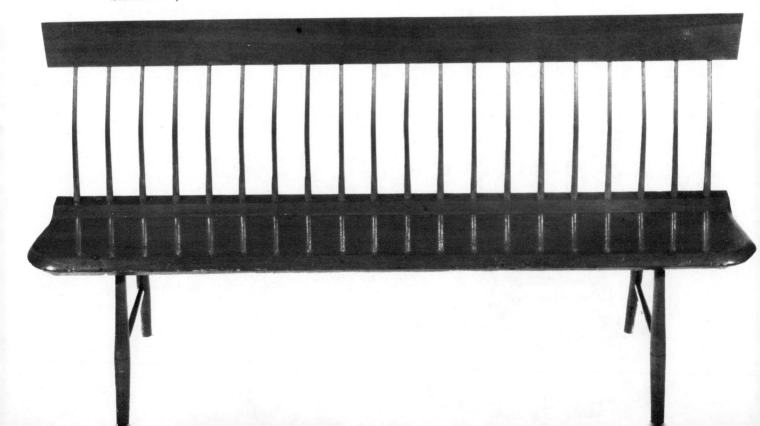

Bow-back Windsor settee was built in Rhode Island between 1750 and 1800. (*Courtesy, Henry Ford Museum*)

Unusual triple-arch, bow-back Windsor settee was made in Connecticut during later years of the 18th century. (*Courtesy, Winterthur Museum*)

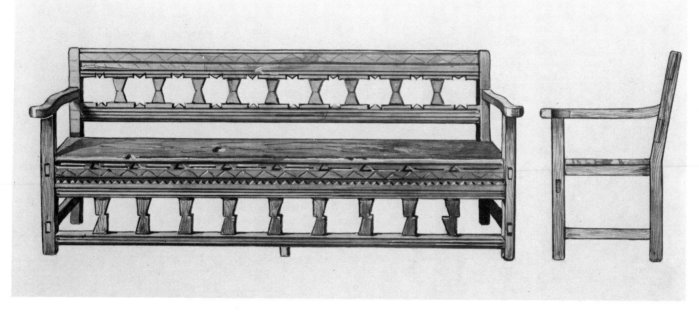

Elongated New Mexico bench, of 18th century origin, reflects both Spanish and Indian mission influences. Note unusual decorative carving. (*Courtesy, Index of American Design*)

Oak sofa, built by Carl Steinhagen in Grimes County, Texas, in 1860, displays opulent details of early Texas German upholstered furniture. (*Courtesy, Winedale Inn, University of Texas at Austin*)

Mission oak sofa, made in Michigan at beginning of the 20th century, shows simplicity of post-Victorian furniture design. (*Courtesy, Henry Ford Museum*)

CHAIR-TABLES & HUTCH-BENCHES

Top Left. Hutch-table, so-called because of built-in chest compartment, has top which swivels on wooden pins. It was built in New York or New England around 1700. (*Courtesy, Index of American Design*)

Top right. Chair-table with oak base was built in Massachusetts between 1680 and 1700. (*Courtesy, Henry Ford Museum*)

Left. French Canadian chair-table (monk's bench) was made in the Province of Quebec late in the 18th century. (*Courtesy, Montreal Museum of Fine Arts*)

Below. Oval-top chair-table originated in New England between 1700 and 1725. (*Courtesy, Winterthur Museum*)

This hutch-table is believed to have been built in the Hudson Valley of New York late in the 18th century. (Courtesy, Sleepy Hollow Restorations)

Hutch-table, built in New Mexico early in the 19th century, shows Spanish and Indian mission influences. Note elaborate tempera decorations. (Courtesy, *Index of American Design*)

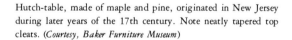

Hutch-table, made of maple and pine, originated in New Jersey during later years of the 17th century. Note neatly tapered top cleats. (Courtesy, *Baker Furniture Museum*)

Bench-table, which follows earlier design, was built at Burlington, Iowa, around 1860. (Courtesy, *Index of American Design*)

95

TABLES

Top left. Ancient trestle table, with pine top and white oak trestles, was made in New England during the 17th century. High rail is unusual for early American tables of this type. (*Courtesy, American Museum in Britain*) See measured drawing, page 150.

Top right. Shaker triple-trestle table of cherry was made in a New England Shaker community around 1840. (*Photographed by author, courtesy, Fruitlands Museums*) See measured drawing, page 153.

Center. French Canadian side table, of 17th century origin, has turned legs and pendants made in the Louis XIII manner. (*Photographed by author, courtesy, Montreal Museum of Fine Arts*) See measured drawing, page 155.

Bottom left. Shaker stretcher table, made at New Lebanon, New York, around 1830, has cherry top and maple legs and stretchers. (*Photographed by author at Hancock, Massachusetts.*)

Bottom right. Tavern table, of 18th century New England origin, has maple legs and pine top. (*Courtesy, Longfellow's Wayside Inn*)

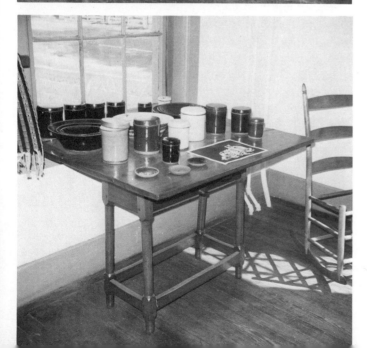

Graceful taper-legged, drop-leaf table was made on a plantation in Clarke County, Alabama, around 1830. *(Courtesy, Carlen House Museum)*

Tavern table with Dutch feet was made in New England late in the 18th century. *(Courtesy, Longfellow's Wayside Inn)*

Shaker dining table was used by the Ministry of the Church Family at Hancock, Massachusetts, around 1830. *(Courtesy, Index of American Design)*

Massive walnut kitchen table was built in Texas during the 19th century. *(Courtesy, Winedale Inn University of Texas at Austin.)*

Top left. Oblong-topped tavern table, of early New England origin, has typical vase and ball-turned legs. (*Courtesy, Longfellow's Wayside Inn*)

Top right. Walnut table, made in Texas in 1860, has cabriole legs and reflects Biedermeir style of European original. (*Courtesy, Winedale Inn, University of Texas at Austin.*)

Center. Spanish influence may be detected in this crude 19th century handmade table, which was found near Santa Fe, New Mexico. (*Courtesy, Index of American Design*)

Bottom left. Split-leg table, made entirely of pine, originated in New England during the 17th century. (*Archive photo*) See measured drawing, page 147.

Bottom right. Spanish gate-leg table, made around 1690, combines pine and walnut to produce this distinguished result. (*Courtesy, St. Augustine Preservation Board*)

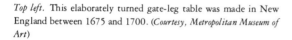

Top left. This elaborately turned gate-leg table was made in New England between 1675 and 1700. (*Courtesy, Metropolitan Museum of Art*)

Top right. Dutch-designed split gate-leg table was made in the Hudson Valley of New York early in the 18th century. (*Photographed by author, Courtesy, Sleepy Hollow Restorations*) See measured drawing, page 169.

Center. French Canadian gate-leg table, with legs turned in the manner of Louis XIII, was made during the 17th century in the Province of Quebec. (*Photographed by author, courtesy, Montreal Museum of Fine Arts*)

Bottom left. Early Norwegian gate-leg table employed squared and pegged legs in lieu of turning. Leaves extend down to floor. (*Courtesy, Vesterheim, Norwegian American Museum*)

Bottom right. Handsome gate-leg table, of early 18th century origin, graces the parlor at Longfellow's Wayside Inn. (*Courtesy, Longfellow's Wayside Inn*)

Top left. Late 17th century oak bedstead, of New England origin, uses rope platform to support bedding. (*Courtesy, Metropolitan Museum of Art*) See measured drawing, page 198.

Center left. Shaker child's bed was made at New Lebanon, New York, around 1840. (*Photographed by author at Hancock, Massachusetts*)

Center right. Yellow pine bed was made by slaves in Louisiana around 1840. (*Courtesy, Index of American Design*)

Bottom left. Norwegian bed and trundle was built in the Decorah region of Iowa around 1855. With no lathes available, squared posts were shaped to simulate turning. (*Courtesy, Vesterheim, Norwegian American Museum*)

Bottom right. Slat-bottom bed, made at Barnesville, Georgia, during mid-19th century, was painted red and has stenciled headboard. (*Courtesy, Atlanta Historical Society*)

Top right. This handsome walnut "cannonball" four-poster bed was made by craftsmen in the Bishop Hill, Illinois, colony between 1846 and 1860. (*Courtesy, Index of American Design*) See measured drawing, page 199.

Center left. Stately four-poster bed was made by slaves in Texas around 1842. (*Courtesy, Index of American Design*)

Center right. Pencil-post four-poster walnut bed was made in Virginia around 1806. (*Courtesy, Index of American Design*)

Bottom left. Elaborately constructed four-poster bed of Empire style was built in a Zoar, Ohio, cabinet shop between 1830 and 1850. (*Courtesy, Index of American Design*)

Bottom right. Longfellow's bedroom at Wayside Inn is furnished with 18th century pieces, including four-poster bed with raw-silk canopy and covers. (*Courtesy, Longfellow's Wayside Inn*)

CRADLES

Top left. Early Pilgrim oak cradle, built between 1625 and 1675, has plain panels with pegged stiles and posts. (*Courtesy, Metropolitan Museum of Art*)

Top right. Elaborately carved cradle, which is believed to date back to 1590, has Renaissance type of incised carving typical of early English cradles. (*Courtesy, Baker Furniture Museum*)

Center. Unusual trestle-suspended cradle, of Dutch Hudson Valley origin, is believed to have been made between 1740 and 1780. (*Courtesy, Winterthur Museum*)

Bottom left. French Canadian hooded cradle was built at St. Barthelemy, Province of Quebec, during early years of the 19th century. (*Courtesy, Montreal Museum of Fine Arts*)

Bottom right. Another early cradle, probably Dutch Hudson Valley origin and dated 1673, has knobs for tying ropes across top to secure infant. (*Courtesy, Sleepy Hollow Restorations*)

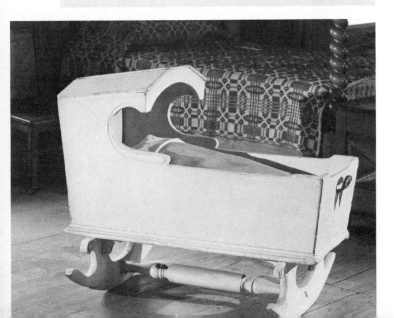

Hooded pine cradle, of 17th century New England origin, is designed to rock on sturdy trestles. (*Courtesy, American Museum in Britain.*) See measured drawing, page 197.

Unusual spindle cradle was made in New England between 1810 and 1840. (*Courtesy, Henry Ford Museum*)

Black stenciled cradle was made commercially in New England during the 18th century. (*Courtesy, Sleepy Hollow Restorations*)

Barrel cradle of pine was made in New England late in the 18th century. (*Courtesy, Sleepy Hollow Restorations*)

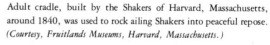

Walnut Pennsylvania German cradle was built between 1750 and 1775. (*Courtesy, Winterthur Museum*)

Adult cradle, built by the Shakers of Harvard, Massachusetts, around 1840, was used to rock ailing Shakers into peaceful repose. (*Courtesy, Fruitlands Museums, Harvard, Massachusetts.*)

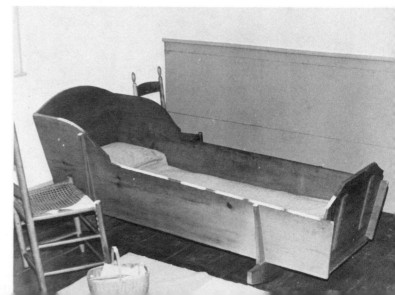

Carved oak blanket chest with pine top. Made between 1660 and 1675, probably at Guilford, Connecticut. (*Courtesy, Index of American Design*)

Painted pine chest, made in Connecticut in 1815. (*Courtesy, Fruitlands Museums*)

Carved pine chest, of 17th century origin, is believed to have been made in New Jersey. (*Courtesy, Henry Ford Museum*)

Native grain chest, made in New Mexico during the 19th century. (*Courtesy, Index of American Design*)

French Canadian chest with painted decorations was made at St. Scholastique, Province of Quebec, late in the 18th century. (*Photographed by author, courtesy, Montreal Museum of Fine Arts*)

Pennsylvania German dowry chest, made in Berks County in 1784. (*Courtesy, Index of American Design*)

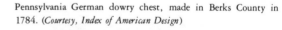

Connecticut painted chest from around 1800. Note individuality of painted motifs. (*Courtesy, Index of American Design*)

Norwegian traveling chest decorated with *rosemaling* and inscribed "1821." (*Courtesy, Little Norway Museum*)

Pennsylvania German dowry chest, inscribed with name *"Christina Ern-stin,"* was made in Lehigh County late in the 18th century. (*Courtesy, Index of American Design*)

Dowry chest, made in Pennsylvania in 1774, is of unusually sturdy construction. (*Courtesy, Winterthur Museum*)

Simply decorated Pennsylvania German dowry chest was made in Lebanon County late in the 18th century. (*Courtesy, Henry Ford Museum*)

Bearing illuminated inscription "Jacob Jutzae — Anno 1781," this Pennsylvania German chest identifies date of its origin. (*Courtesy, Index of American Design*)

Pine desk on frame was made between 1680 and 1700. Although it made its way to New England, it is believed to be of Scandinavian origin. *(Archive photo)* See measured drawing, page 186.

Provincial version of classical New England drop-lid desk was made in the South toward the end of the 18th century. Note bracket feet and turned drawer knobs. *(Archive photo)* See measured drawing, page 187.

Graceful scrutoire was made in the Hudson Valley of New York around 1785. *(Courtesy, Sleepy Hollow Restorations)*

French Canadian desk, of bird's-eye maple, has fold-up counter and shelves for books in top cabinet. *(Courtesy, National Gallery of Canada)*

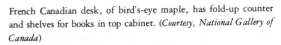

This delicate little Shaker desk is believed to have been made at Hancock, Massachusetts, around 1840. (*Courtesy, New York State Museum*)

Norwegian drop-lid desk was built in a rural area near Fergus Falls, Minnesota, around 1870. Note Norwegian *kubbestol* beside desk. (*Courtesy, Vesterheim, Norwegian American Museum*)

Texas secretary desk, made by slaves on plantation at Upper Red River in 1820, has ample space for storing books and records. (*Courtesy, Index of American Design*)

This plantation desk was built in rural Georgia during early years of the 19th century. (*Courtesy, Atlanta Historical Society*)

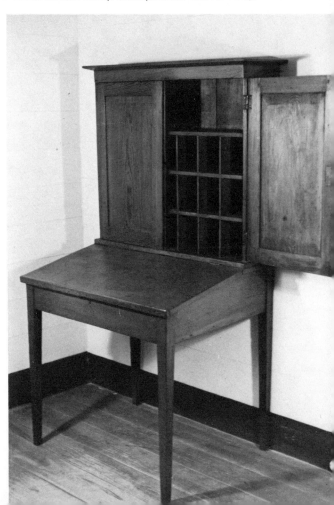

CHESTS OF DRAWERS

Top left. Oak two-drawer chest, with applied geometrical moldings and split turning decorations, was made in New England between 1675 and 1700. (*Courtesy, Index of American Design*)

Top right. Elaborately carved and initialed Hadley chest was made in Connecticut during later years of the 17th century. (*Courtesy, Index of American Design*)

Center. Painted chest of drawers, dated 1731, is decorated with birds and rosettes. Note teardrop drawer pulls. (*Courtesy, Index of American Design*)

Below left. Highly decorated chest of drawers was built at Guilford, Connecticut, around 1700. (*Courtesy, Index of American Design*)

Below right. This more advanced Connecticut chest of drawers displays turned turnip feet and symmetrically arranged thistle decorations. It was made early in the 18th century. (*Courtesy, Index of American Design*)

This sturdy Empire-inspired chest of drawers was built at Bastrop, Texas, around 1850. (*Courtesy, Winedale Inn, University of Texas at Austin.*)

Tall pine chest of drawers was made by Massachusetts Shakers around 1850. (*Courtesy, Henry Ford Museum*)

Detailed view of painted decorations applied to early Connecticut chests of drawers. Note how floral motifs blend but vary in design from drawer to drawer. (*Courtesy, Index of American Design*)

Mahogany chest of drawers was made on the Randall Plantation at Huntsville, Texas, prior to 1860. (*Courtesy, Index of American Design*)

Red stained chest, with one drawer, was made by Shakers of New Lebanon, New York, in 1836. (*Courtesy, Index of American Design*)

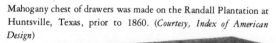

CUPBOARDS

Top Left. French Canadian *armoirette,* of 18th century origin, has plain paneled door secured with wooden latch. (*Courtesy, Musée du Quebec*)

Top right. Louis XIII-inspired French Canadian cupboard, with diamond-point paneled door, was made near the end of the 17th century. (*Courtesy, Musée du Quebec*)

Center. Connecticut pine cupboard from the 18th century. Note back slant of top, which resembles ship's cupboard. (*Courtesy, Sleepy Hollow Restorations*)

Bottom left. Tall Shaker chest of drawers with cupboard top was made in Massachusetts around the middle of the 19th century. (*Courtesy, Index of American Design*)

Bottom right. Cypress cupboard was made at Yorktown, Texas, around 1860. (*Courtesy, Index of American Design*)

Sturdy corner cupboard, made in Pennsylvania during early years of the 18th century, has sides and shelves made of pine boards a full one inch thick. (*Courtesy, Philadelphia Museum of Art*) See measured drawing of similar design, page 203.

Spanish pie safe, or *confessionario* (so-called because grilling resembled doors of church confessional), was a basic requirement in most Spanish-speaking countries. This one was built at Catalonia, Spain, around 1820. (*Courtesy, St. Augustine Preservation Board*) See measured drawing, page 202.

Open pine cupboard, made in Massachusetts during the 17th century, has fine cyma-scrolled front facing. (*Courtesy, Index of American Design*)

Cupboard with plate rack was built at Beaumont, Quebec, during the 18th century. Note Louis XV paneled doors and unusual strap hinges. (*Courtesy, Montreal Museum of Fine Arts*)

French Canadian two-tiered buffet cupboard, with broken pediment crown, was made in the Renaissance and Louis XIII manners. Built during the 18th century, this cupboard displays the finest French Canadian craftsmanship. Note the deep carving of diamond-point door panels. (*Courtesy, Montreal Museum of Fine Arts*)

Another French Canadian buffet cupboard shows influence of Louis XV design. This one was made near the end of the 18th century. Note unusual scrolled design of door panels. (*Courtesy, Musée du Quebec*)

BUFFETS, DRESSERS & WARDROBES

Massive Dutch *kas,* with elaborate grisaille painted decorations, is reminiscent of *trompe l'oeil* paintings in Dutch homes of the 17th century. These highly decorative two-door cabinets were the prized possessions of early Dutch settlers. (*Courtesy, Index of American Design*)

This glazed china cupboard was made in Colorado County, Texas, around 1870. Note fine proportions and skilled craftsmanship of construction. (*Courtesy, Winedale Inn, University of Texas at Austin*)

Small glazed buffet cupboard, decorated with circular incised *galettes* in the Breton manner, originated in Quebec, Canada, early in the 19th century. (*Courtesy, National Museum of Man*)

Painted Dutch cupboard imitates the patroon school of painting in its portrayal of biblical scenes on the front and grisaille side panels. This interesting cupboard was built in the Hudson Valley of New York around 1700. (*Photographed by author, courtesy, Sleepy Hollow Restorations*)

Louis XV armoire was made in Canada around 1800. This large piece is beautifully constructed, giving artistic attention to details of decorative scrolled paneling. (*Courtesy, National Gallery of Canada*)

Early *Armoire à L'Ancienne*, made in the Louis XIII manner, originated in Canada late in the 17th century. The deep diamond-point carved panels give the impression that several chests were placed upon one another. (*Courtesy, Montreal Museum of Fine Arts*)

OTHER DESIGNS

Top Left. Shaker medicine chest made at Pleasant Hill, Kentucky, around 1830. (*Courtesy, Index of American Design*)

Top right. Hanging corner cupboard, dated around 1880, was designed and made by Sven Bergstrom of Scandia, Minnesota. (*Courtesy, Index of American Design*)

Center. Comb and brush rack was made by Rufus Hutchins at Waubeek, Iowa, around 1860. (*Courtesy, Index of American Design*)

Bottom left. Shaker kitchen cupboard was built at Harvard, Massachusetts, around 1840. (*Courtesy, Fruitlands Museums*)

Bottom right. Pine wall shelves were made in New England late in the 18th century. (*Courtesy, Sleepy Hollow Restorations*)

Top left. Norwegian corner cupboard, or *skop,* was built in 1859. (*Courtesy, Little Norway Museum*)

Top right. Set of pine wall shelves was made in New England in 1825. (*Courtesy, Fruitlands Museums*)

Center. Portable secretary in Hepplewhite style was made in Philadelphia between 1770 and 1780. (*Courtesy, Index of American Design*)

Bottom left. Windsor "cricket" footstool, of painted pine and maple, was made in New England between 1775 and 1800. (*Courtesy, Henry Ford Museum*)

Bottom right. Pantry at Phillipsburg Manor displays early Dutch dough box, assorted pegleg stools and X-trestle tables. Hanging on the wall are various kitchen tools and accessories. (*Courtesy, Sleepy Hollow Restorations*)

Surgeon's field desk, dated 1861, was used by Belitha Powell, chief surgeon of the Trans-Mississippi Department of the Confederate States of America. (*Courtesy, Index of American Design*)

Saddler's workbench was made by slaves at the Midnight Plantation, Lake Village, Arkansas, around 1855. (*Courtesy, Index of American Design*)

Cobbler's bench was made around 1825 in Pennsylvania. Note sturdy construction of bottom rail bracing. (*Courtesy, Index of American Design*)

III COUNTRY CONSTRUCTION

All antique country furniture has a common denominator of sturdy construction. Whether the piece was influenced by Spanish, Dutch, English, French, German or Scandinavian design, the solid-wood construction remained essentially the same. This involved the use of strong wood joints, usually reinforced with hardwood pegs. Since furniture made during the early years of America was seldom joined with glue, dovetails, wooden pegs and keyed tenons were needed to secure its assembly.

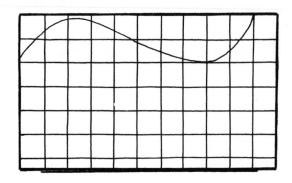

Some of the more elaborate pieces shown in this book required craft skills exceeding those needed to produce the simpler provincial pieces. Such skills were developed by traditional joiner's guilds abroad and were brought to America by professional furniture makers. However, much of the work shown on these pages was of elementary construction — and made by rural carpenters.

Template Transfers of Scrollwork

A *template,* or full-scale pattern, is used to mark scrolls. It is made with a piece of cardboard marked in one-inch squares. On these squares the intersections of curved lines are spotted from graphed areas of scrollwork shown in measured drawings. The scrolled pattern is produced by connecting the marked spots with free-flowing lines and then cutting the template with scissors. When the scroll curve is reciprocal, as with the double cyma shown at right, a half-template is made and pivoted on a center line to mark the full pattern.

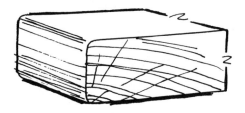

Edge Shapes

Tops of tables, chests and benches were usually shaped along the edges with distinctive edge molding. Sometimes this was extremely plain — consisting only of dulled edges. But for other types and nationalities of work, more ornate shapes were employed. Of the typical assortment of edge shapes shown at the right, several were produced with straight-cutting planes and abrasive tools. The more elaborate shapes, however, had to be made with molding planes with specially ground cutters.

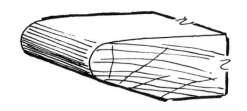

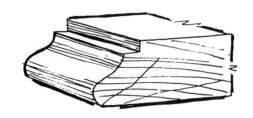

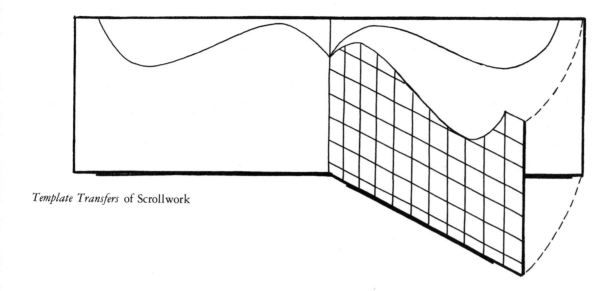

Template Transfers of Scrollwork

Edge Shapes

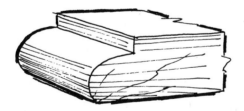

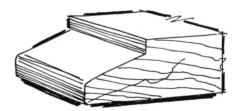

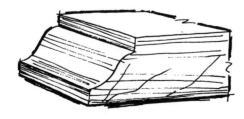

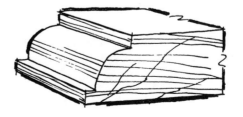

Applied Moldings

Like the edge shapes previously shown, a vast variety of applied moldings were used to decorate early country furniture. These were made in strips of various shapes and thicknesses. All were distinctively shaped — ranging from the simple beaded types to heavy cornice trimmings.

The hand processes required for making such moldings involved the use of molding planes with specially ground cutters. The shape was first planed on the edge of a board, and then the strip was sawed off to produce the molding. The strips were then applied to the work with small nails and glue.

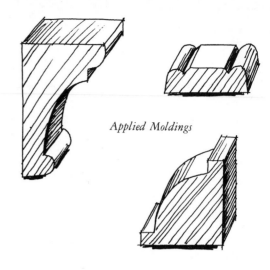

Applied Moldings

End Cleats

To prevent the warping of broad board surfaces, separate cleats were sometimes fastened to the ends of table tops, cabinets and chests. These were attached with hardwood pegs or, more frequently, with tongue-and-groove and mortise-and-tenon joints, as shown at right. Before glues were available, pegs were used to reinforce all joints. In modern production, end cleats are generally tongue-and-grooved and permanently glued.

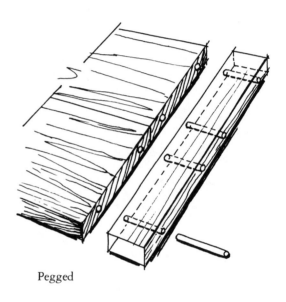

Pegged

Edge Joints

The job of joining boards together to produce broad surfaces must have been formidable before the advent of modern woodworking machinery. Some of the methods employed for edge-joining table tops of antique country furniture are shown at right. These include simple butt fastenings, as well as the more complicated processes of doweling, tongue and grooving, rabbeting, splining and inlaying with hardwood butterfly fasteners. The last method was used before reliable glues became available.

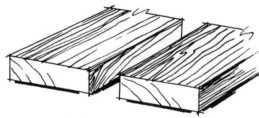

Butt-Fastened

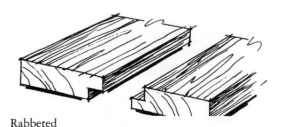

Rabbeted

120

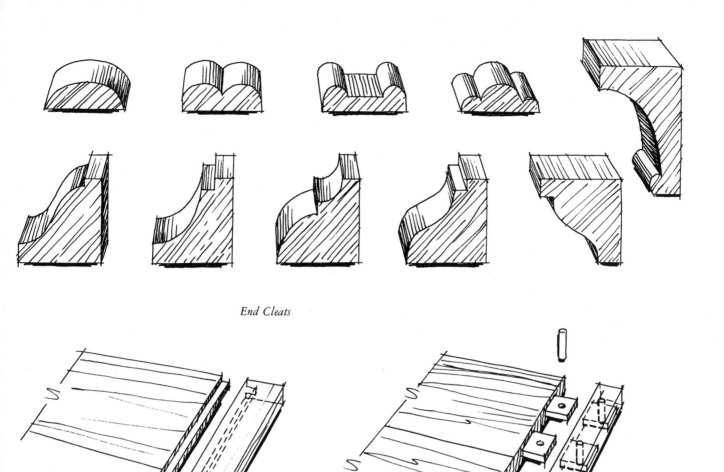

End Cleats

Tongue-and-Grooved

Mortise-and-Tenoned

Edge Joints

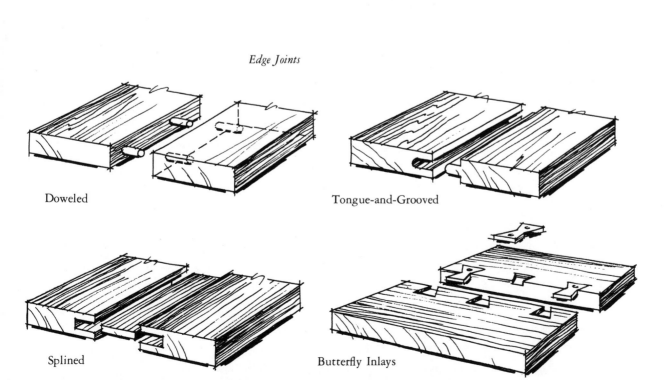

Doweled

Tongue-and-Grooved

Splined

Butterfly Inlays

Dado Joints

Dadoes are grooves cut across the grain of a board. They are usually used for shelf construction. They may be either *open* — with the groove exposed at the intersection of shelf and attached member — or *closed,* — with the groove inset from the front edge of the connecting piece. Another method is to cut a tenon on the connecting piece, which fits into the inset dado groove. Both of the concealed dado techniques are called *blind dadoes.*

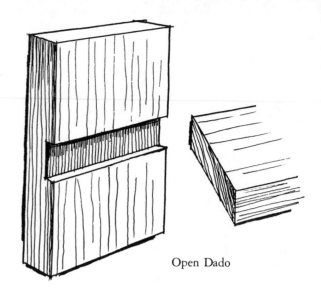

Open Dado

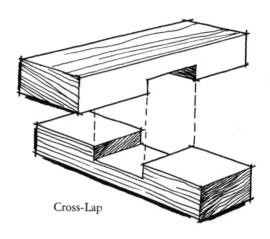

Cross-Lap

Lapped Joints

To make bases for stands and stemmed tables, as well as frames, the early craftsmen frequently employed lapped joints. As shown at the right, these included reciprocating *cross-laps,* *end-laps* and *middle-laps.* They were made by cutting away half of the wood of two connecting pieces and fitting the cutout portions together to form a flush connection. Usually, this connection was reinforced with glue, screws or nails.

Lapped joints, accurately cut, contributed additional strength to furniture construction. As illustrated at right, they were especially used for the bases of early candlestands. In this construction, after the cross-laps were cut and fitted, the craftsman proceeded to cut the scrolled shape of the foot design. When the foot shapes were smoothed to pattern, the cross-lapped base was permanently joined together and then bored at the center to receive the stem tenon.

Cross-Lap Base Construction

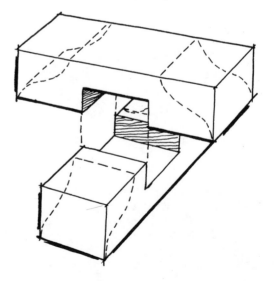

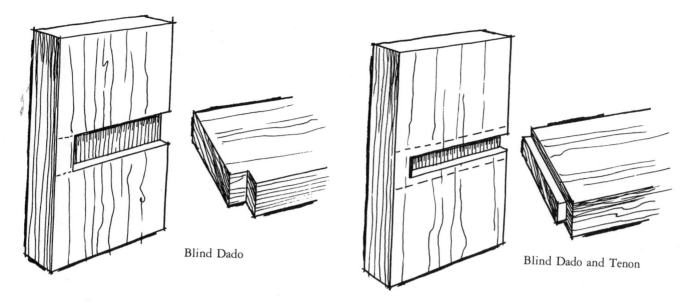

Blind Dado

Blind Dado and Tenon

Dado Joints

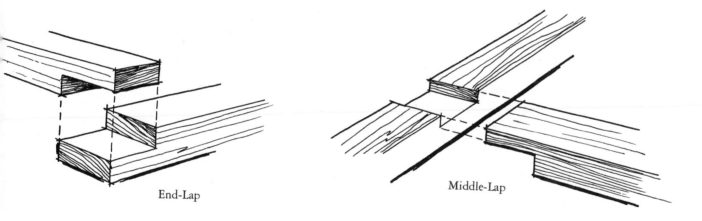

End-Lap

Middle-Lap

Lapped Joints

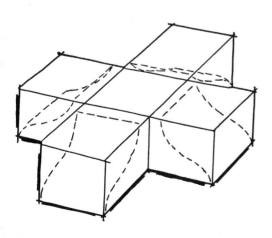

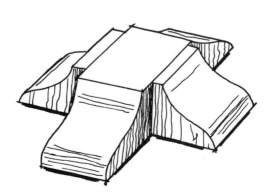

Dovetail Joints

Dovetail joints were a favorite of early woodworkers — and were widely used by all nationalities in the making of antique country furniture. Aside from their neatness of appearance, their exceptional strength and durability caused them to be used for many types of construction.

Basically, there are two types of dovetail joints — *open* and *concealed*. In drawer construction both types are usually employed. As shown at right, open dovetails are made with each connecting member fully overlapping the other at the connection. But for concealed dovetails, the side members must be inset to occupy a marginal portion of the connecting edge. Thus, when the drawer is closed, the dovetail joints remain invisible. As illustrated here, in drawer construction open dovetails are used at the back of the drawer, while concealed dovetails are used at the front where they can be seen from the side only when the drawer is opened.

Old chests, boxes, desks and cabinets frequently employed open dovetails for corner construction. The types of dovetails varied in shape. Some articles used a single dovetail, while others showed equally spaced multiple dovetails. For neatness of appearance, many pieces were made with *feathered* dovetails, in which the size of the overlapping sections exceeded that of the slim, feathered slivers into which they were fitted.

Honesty of construction, as exposed on the open-dovetailed corner of the chest shown at right, enhances these articles in the eyes of present-day antique admirers. The craftsmanlike handwork they display adds a nostalgic note to their treasured antiquity.

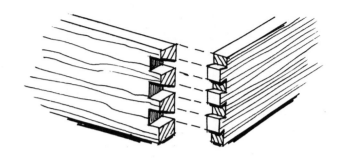

Open Dovetails

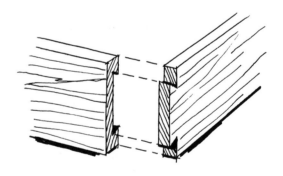

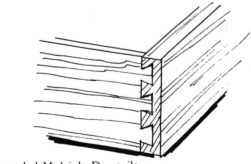

Concealed Multiple Dovetails

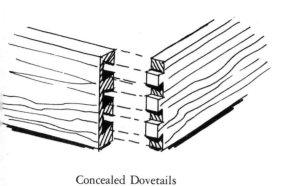

Concealed Dovetails

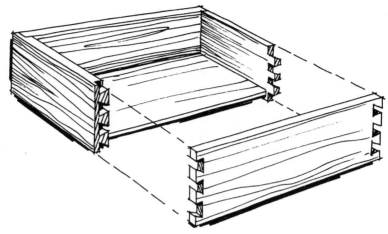

Dovetailed Drawer Construction

Dovetail Joints

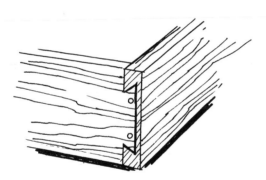

Concealed Single Dovetail

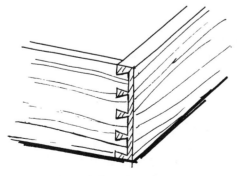

Concealed Feathered Dovetails

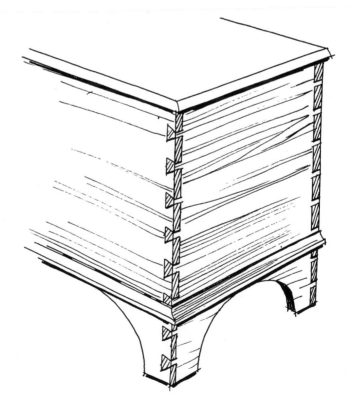

Open Dovetailed Chest Construction

Dovetailed Construction

The dovetail form was also used for several other types of early construction. As shown at the right, it offered the advantage of joining wooden parts together in such a way as to prevent their being pulled apart. Thus, dovetailed tenons were particularly effective for joining legs to the stems of pedestal tables, where the pressure of gravity would otherwise separate the connecting parts. For shelf construction, both open and concealed *sliding* dovetailed dadoes were used to hold the joining parts firmly together. Such construction was essential for early joinery before adequate glues became available to secure the connecting parts.

For bracing benches, the Shakers used a distinctive type of *half-dovetail*, which was fitted into cutouts of the connecting members. Reinforced with nails, such bracing provided a firm fix of parts, preventing any possibility of connecting members working loose. Another type of half-dovetail joint was often used to secure heavier constructions. This was cut like a middle-lap joint, but the dovetailed shape of the lapped portion prevented the connecting pieces from pulling apart.

Hinged Joints

Three types of hinged joints were used to secure the leaves of early drop-leaf tables. Of these, the *plain butt joint* was most common. The *tongue-and-groove* hinged joint was also widely used, as well as the *rule joint,* which was the neatest. With all three types, the butt hinges were mortised in flush to the undersurfaces of the leaves and the top.

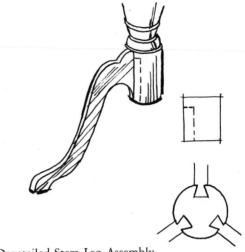

Dovetailed Stem-Leg Assembly

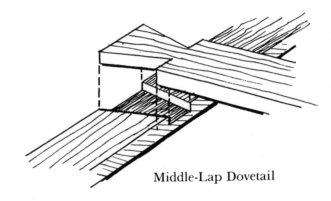

Middle-Lap Dovetail

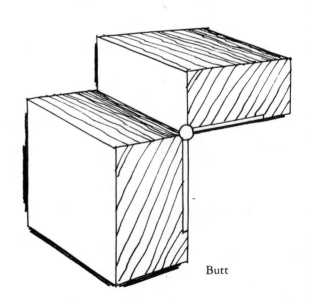

Butt

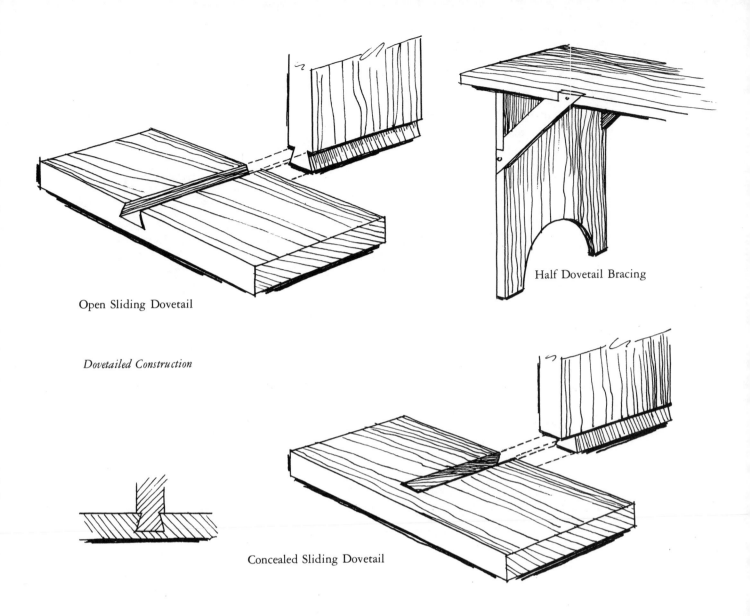

Open Sliding Dovetail

Half Dovetail Bracing

Dovetailed Construction

Concealed Sliding Dovetail

Hinged Joints

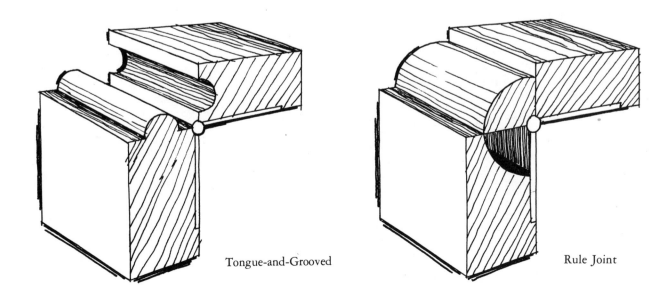

Tongue-and-Grooved

Rule Joint

Mortise-&-Tenon Joints

Since time immemorial, mortise-and-tenon joints have been used to connect parts of furniture. These have been made in various ways, depending on the practices of regional craftsmen. Before strong glues became available, the mortise-and-tenon joint was most frequently reinforced with hardwood pegs. This was done according to the *drawbore-pin* method, which involved boring a hole one-eighth inch nearer the *tenon* shoulder than a corresponding hole bored through the mortised member. Thus, when the hardwood peg was pounded in place, the tenon was drawn snugly within the mortise.

Haunched mortise-and-tenon joints were used for paneled constructions where an inside groove was first cut to receive the panel. In most early work the tenons were cut long enough to penetrate entirely through the connecting mortise. These through-tenons were usually further strengthened with hardwood wedges driven into slots at their ends. The wedges spread the tenons to produce an enduring joint.

Old trestle tables were usually made with cross-rail tenons piercing the end posts and protruding beyond the mortise. The rails were secured with tapered keys driven either horizontally or vertically through the protruding end of the tenon. As the tapered key was driven into place, the post was drawn snugly against the shoulders of the protruding tenon. This was sometimes varied by using a rail without tenons but secured on *both* sides of the post mortise with keyed wedges.

All types of mortise-and-tenon joints were designed to contribute to the long life of the furniture on which they were used. Examination of sturdy old chairs and tables in museums throughout the country offers ample testimony to the strength and endurance of this construction, applied centuries ago by the craftsmen of that era.

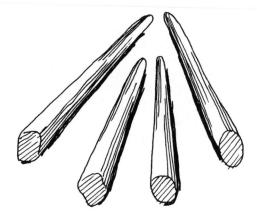

Hardwood Pegs

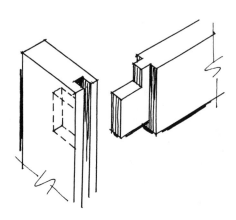

Haunched Mortise-and-Tenon

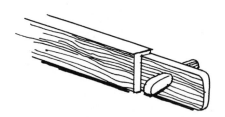

Horizontal-Keyed Tenon

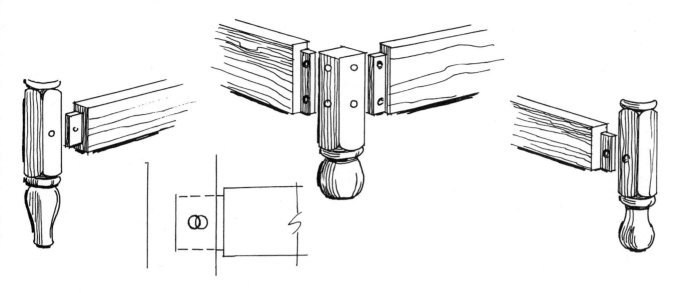

Drawbore-Pin, Pegged Mortise-and-Tenon Construction

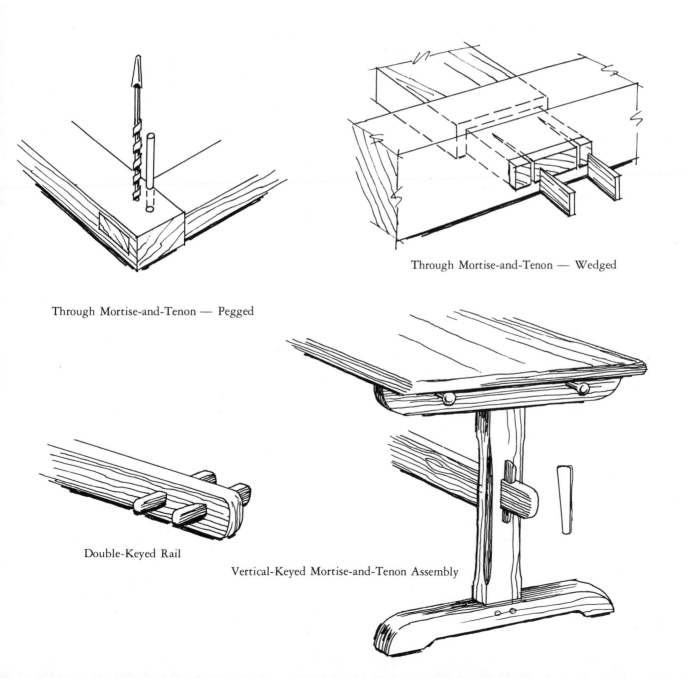

Through Mortise-and-Tenon — Wedged

Through Mortise-and-Tenon — Pegged

Double-Keyed Rail

Vertical-Keyed Mortise-and-Tenon Assembly

Cabriole Legs

Many of the baroque designs shown in this book require cabriole legs. To shape such legs, dual cutting operations are required, involving the use of template patterns of the leg design. First, the leg is mortised in square form, and then a cardboard template of the shape is made and traced on the squared leg. After the shape has been cut and smoothed on one side, the template is again used to mark the shape on the curved edges. With the final cutting to shape, the finished cabriole leg is smoothed with abrasive tools to obtain the desired flowing curves.

In attaching the legs to the tenoned rails, it may be desirable to cut the curved shape of the rail *after* the connection has been secured. In this way the continuous flow of the curve from legs to rail may be more easily shaped. A small portion of the tenon shoulder of the rail may be left uncut until after the joint has been secured. This portion is then removed with a saw, and the assembly is smoothed into shape.

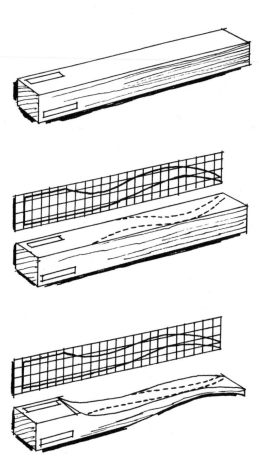

Marking Templates of Leg Shape

Pegleg Construction

Many of the old stools and benches simply required peglegs, which were mortised into the top. Usually, this was performed with a boring block, prebored to the desired leg slant. The boring block was then clamped to the corners of the top, and holes were bored through to receive the leg tenons. Usually, the tenons were split with slots to receive hardwood wedges. These were driven in to spread the tenon and secure the assembly of legs and top. Sometimes, when the tenon did not fully penetrate the top, the holes were bored only partway through. For this assembly the tenons were slotted to receive wedges, which expanded the tenon when the legs were driven into the top holes.

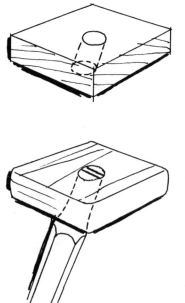

Smoothing to Cabriole Shape

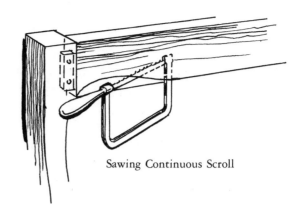

Sawing Continuous Scroll

Cabriole Legs

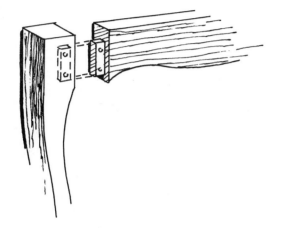

Direct Mortise-and-Tenon Assembly of Legs and Rail

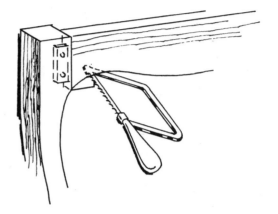

Sawing Rail Scroll After Assembly

Pegleg Construction

Boring and Assembling Pegleg Mortise-and-Tenon

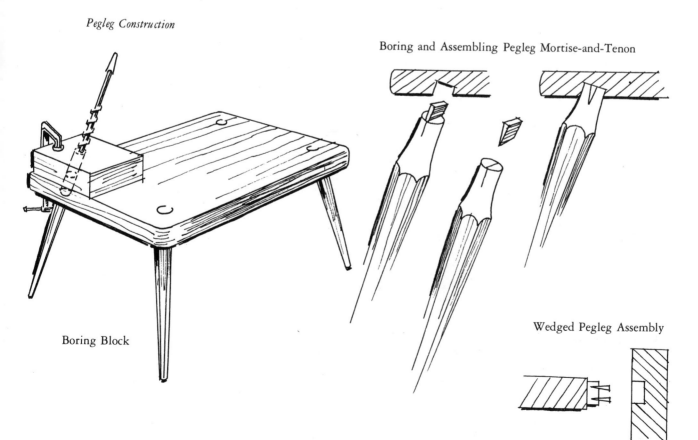

Boring Block

Wedged Pegleg Assembly

Scrolled Paneling

Doors and sides of French cabinets were frequently decorated with scrolled panels. These were framed in the ordinary way with pegged mortise-and-tenon joints. But before being assembled, the rails were shaped with templates of the scrolls and then grooved to receive the panels. After the panels were shaped to scrolled patterns, the edges were usually chamfered and tapered into a thin border in order to fit within the grooves of the connecting stiles and rails. To allow for subsequent swelling of the panels, they were made slightly smaller than the depths of the grooves into which they were fitted. Sometimes scrolled-panel effects were simulated with decorative outlines incised on solid panels.

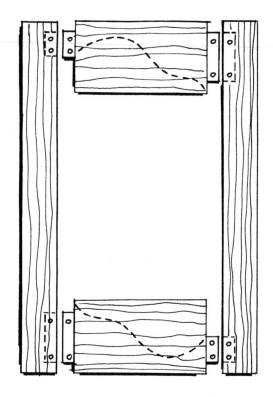

Mortise-and-Tenon Construction of Frame

Turning with Templates

In order to accurately interpret turned patterns, old (as well as new) craftsmen undoubtedly started with full-scale templates of the turned designs. These are graphed on one-inch squares, following the exact patterns graphed on the measured drawings. The graphed template is then mounted on the wall, directly behind the lathe, and constantly checked with ruler and calipers as the turning process proceeds. Needless to say, the accuracy with which the template is graphed determines the final precision of the turning. So, care should be taken to interpret the shapes exactly from the measured drawing.

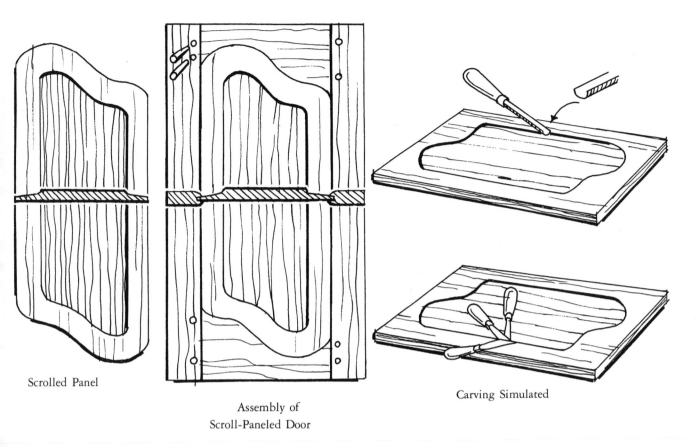

Scrolled Panel

Assembly of
Scroll-Paneled Door

Carving Simulated

Scrolled Paneling

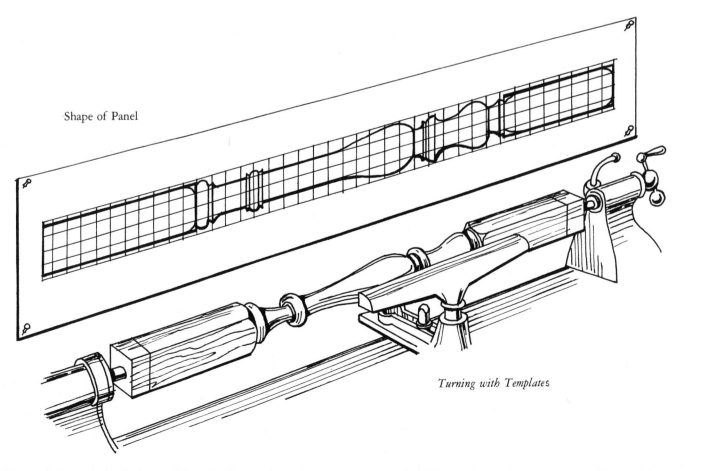

Shape of Panel

Turning with Templates

IV MEASURED DRAWINGS OF COUNTRY CLASSICS

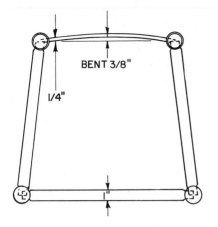

BENT 3/8"

1/4"

1"

SLAT-BACK SIDE CHAIR
New England, about 1700. (*Courtesy, Longfellow's Wayside Inn*)

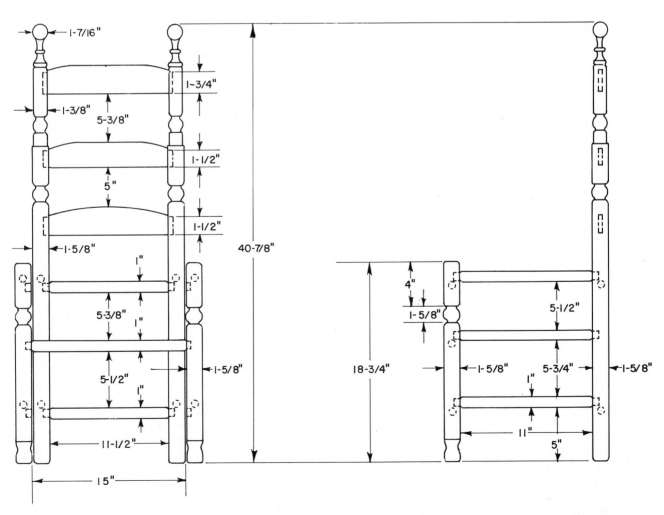

1-7/16"

1-3/4"

1-3/8"

5-3/8"

1-1/2"

5"

1-1/2"

1-5/8"

1"

40-7/8"

5-3/8"

1"

5-1/2"

1"

1-5/8"

11-1/2"

15"

4"

1-5/8"

5-1/2"

18-3/4"

1-5/8"

5-3/4"

1-5/8"

1"

11"

5"

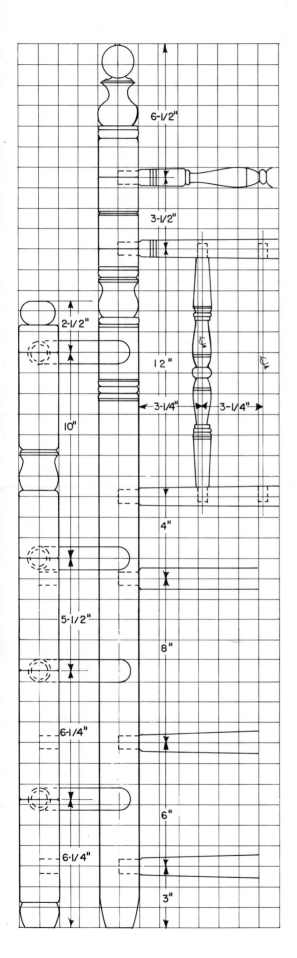

6-1/2"

3-1/2"

2-1/2"

12"

10"

3-1/4" ← → 3-1/4"

4"

5-1/2"

8"

6-1/4"

6"

6-1/4"

3"

GOVERNOR CARVER ARMCHAIR
New England, about 1650–1700. (*Courtesy,
Metropolitan Museum of Art*)

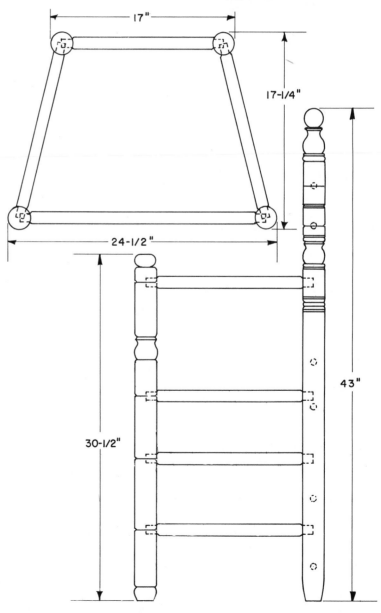

17"

17-1/4"

24-1/2"

30-1/2"

43"

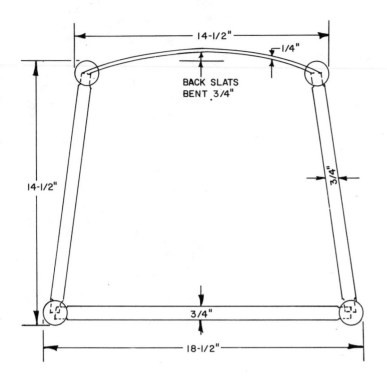

14-1/2"

1/4"

BACK SLATS
BENT 3/4"

3/4"

14-1/2"

3/4"

18-1/2"

SHAKER DINING CHAIR

Niskeyuna, New York, about 1830. (*Photographed by author at The Shaker Museum, Old Chatham*)

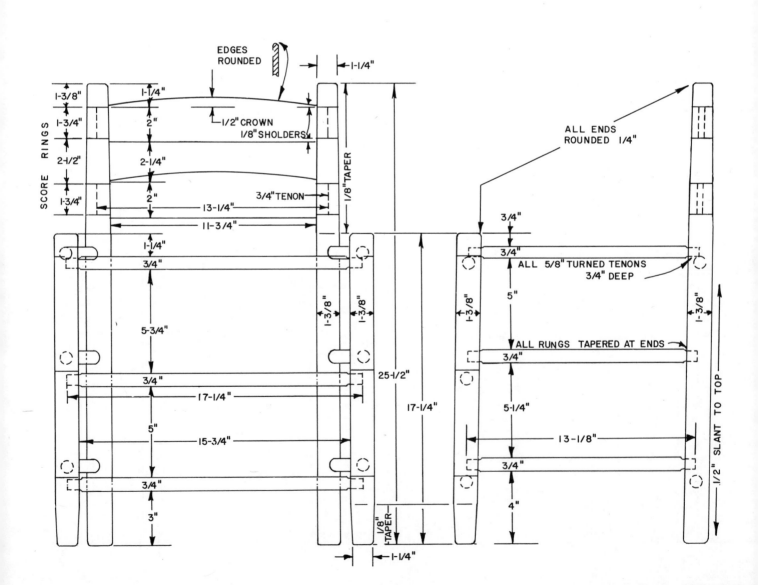

EDGES
ROUNDED

1-1/4"

1-3/8"

1-1/4"

1-3/4"

2"

1/2" CROWN
1/8" SHOLDERS

SCORE RINGS

2-1/2"

2-1/4"

1/8" TAPER

1-3/4"

2"

3/4" TENON

13-1/4"

11-3/4"

ALL ENDS
ROUNDED 1/4"

1-1/4"

3/4"

1-3/8"

1-3/8"

3/4"

3/4"

ALL 5/8" TURNED TENONS
3/4" DEEP

5-3/4"

5"

1-3/8"

1-3/8"

25-1/2"

3/4"

17-1/4"

ALL RUNGS TAPERED AT ENDS

3/4"

5"

17-1/4"

15-3/4"

5-1/4"

13-1/8"

3/4"

3/4"

3"

1/8" TAPER

1-1/4"

4"

1/2" SLANT TO TOP

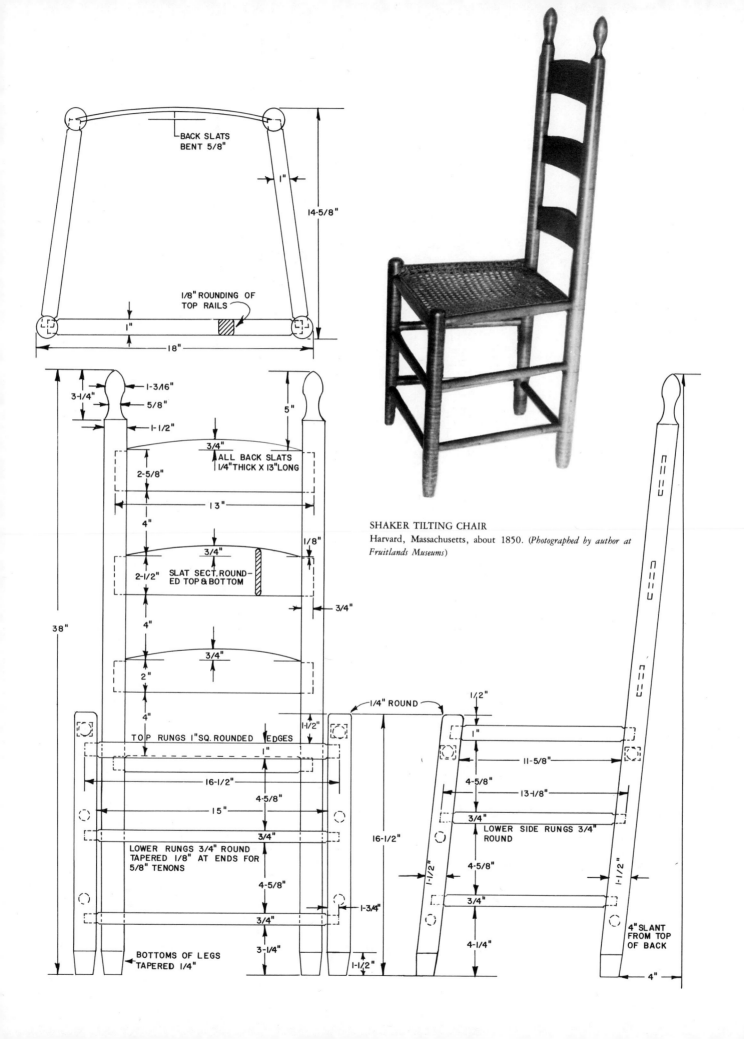

BACK SLATS
BENT 5/8"

1"

14-5/8"

1/8" ROUNDING OF
TOP RAILS

1"

18"

1-3/16"
3-1/4"
5/8"
1-1/2"
5"
3/4"
ALL BACK SLATS
1/4" THICK X 13" LONG
2-5/8"
13"
4"
1/8"
3/4"
SLAT SECT. ROUND-
ED TOP & BOTTOM
2-1/2"
3/4"
4"
3/4"
3/4"
2"
38"
4"
1-1/2"
1/2"
1/4" ROUND
TOP RUNGS 1" SQ. ROUNDED EDGES
1"
1"
16-1/2"
11-5/8"
4-5/8"
4-5/8"
15"
13-1/8"
3/4"
3/4"
LOWER SIDE RUNGS 3/4"
ROUND
16-1/2"
LOWER RUNGS 3/4" ROUND
TAPERED 1/8" AT ENDS FOR
5/8" TENONS
4-5/8"
4-5/8"
3/4"
3/4"
1-3/4"
1-1/2"
4-1/4"
BOTTOMS OF LEGS
TAPERED 1/4"
3-1/4"
1-1/2"
4" SLANT
FROM TOP
OF BACK
4"

SHAKER TILTING CHAIR

Harvard, Massachusetts, about 1850. (*Photographed by author at Fruitlands Museums*)

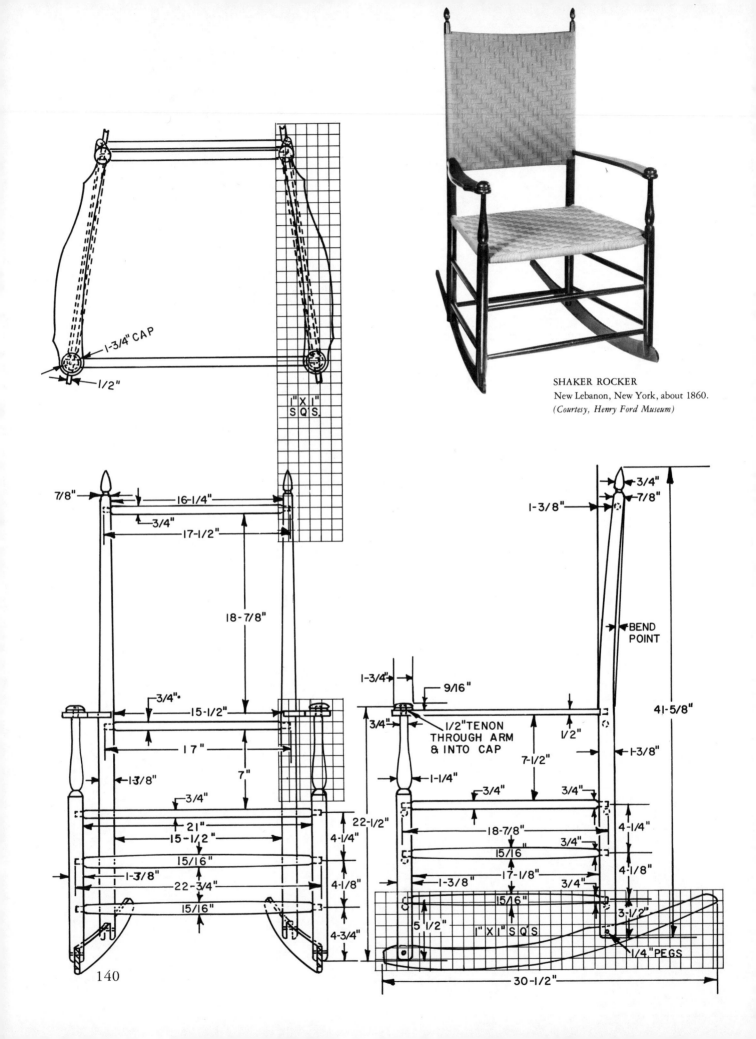

1-3/4" CAP

1/2"

1" X 1" SQS.

SHAKER ROCKER
New Lebanon, New York, about 1860.
(*Courtesy, Henry Ford Museum*)

7/8"

16-1/4"

3/4"

17-1/2"

18-7/8"

3/4"

15-1/2"

17"

7"

1-3/8"

3/4"

21"

15-1/2"

15/16"

1-3/8"

22-3/4"

15/16"

4-3/4"

140

3/4"

7/8"

1-3/8"

BEND POINT

41-5/8"

1-3/8"

1-3/4"

9/16"

3/4"

1/2" TENON THROUGH ARM & INTO CAP

1/2"

7-1/2"

1-1/4"

3/4"

3/4"

18-7/8"

15/16"

3/4"

1-3/8"

17-1/8"

3/4"

15/16"

5 1/2"

1" X 1" SQS.

1/4" PEGS

30-1/2"

22-1/2"

4-1/4"

4-1/8"

4-1/4"

4-1/8"

3-1/2"

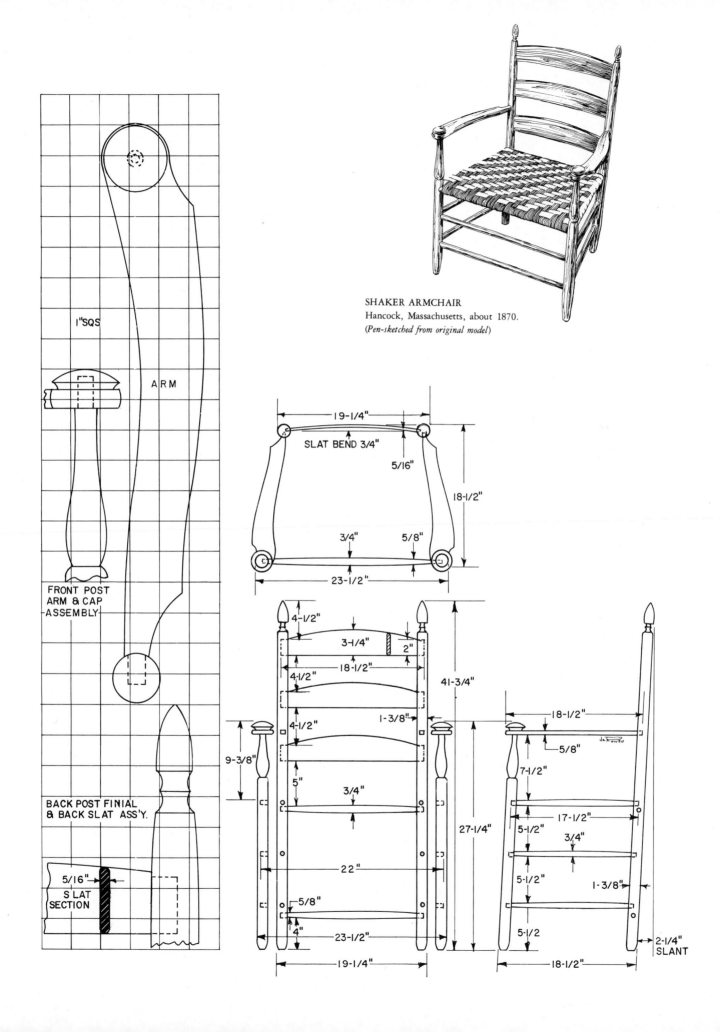

I"SQS

ARM

FRONT POST
ARM & CAP
ASSEMBLY

BACK POST FINIAL
& BACK SLAT ASS'Y.

5/16"

SLAT
SECTION

SHAKER ARMCHAIR
Hancock, Massachusetts, about 1870.
(Pen-sketched from original model)

19-1/4"

SLAT BEND 3/4"

5/16"

18-1/2"

3/4"   5/8"

23-1/2"

4-1/2"

3-1/4"   2"

18-1/2"

4-1/2"

41-3/4"

1-3/8"

4-1/2"

9-3/8"

5"

3/4"

27-1/4"

22"

5/8"

4"

23-1/2"

19-1/4"

18-1/2"

5/8"

7-1/2"

17-1/2"

5-1/2"   3/4"

5-1/2"

1-3/8"

5-1/2

18-1/2"

2-1/4"
SLANT

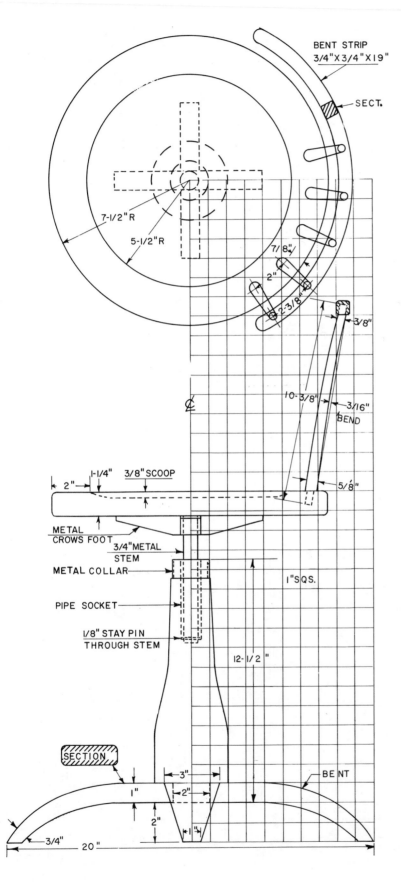

BENT STRIP
3/4"X3/4"X19"

SECT.

7-1/2"R

5-1/2"R

7/8"

2"

2-3/8"

3/8"

10-3/8"

3/16"
BEND

5/8"

1-1/4"   3/8"SCOOP

2"

METAL
CROWS FOOT

3/4"METAL
STEM

METAL COLLAR

PIPE SOCKET

1/8" STAY PIN
THROUGH STEM

1"SQS.

12-1/2"

SECTION

3"

BENT

1"

2"

2"

1"

3/4"   20"

SHAKER REVOLVING STOOL
New Lebanon, New York, about 1840. (*Photographed by author at
The Shaker Museum, Old Chatham*)

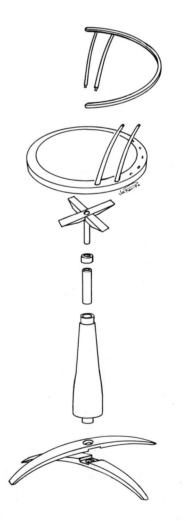

NEW ENGLAND SETTLE

Massachusetts, about 1660. (*Pen-sketched from photograph furnished by The Metropolitan Museum of Art*)

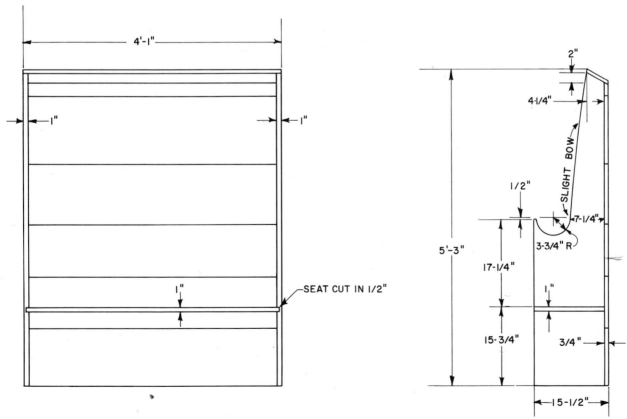

4'-1"

1"   1"

1"

SEAT CUT IN 1/2"

2"

4-1/4"

SLIGHT BOW

1/2"

7-1/4"

3-3/4" R

5'-3"

17-1/4"

1"

15-3/4"

3/4"

15-1/2"

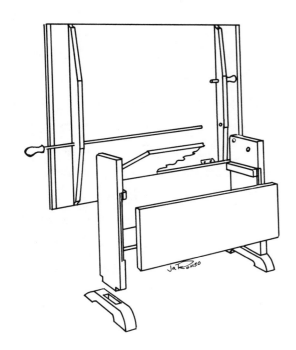

HUTCH-TABLE
Marblehead, Massachusetts, early 18th century. (*Pen-sketched from museum photograph*)

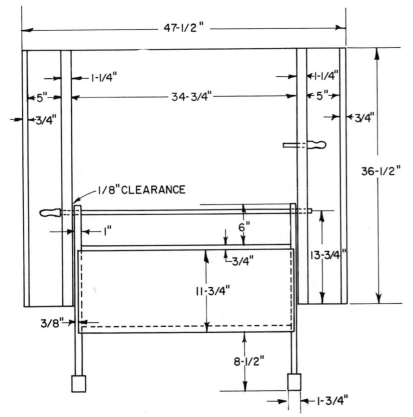

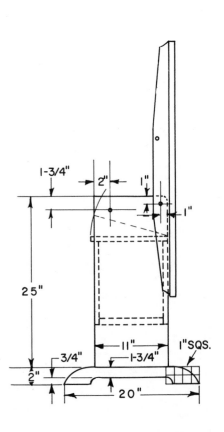

144

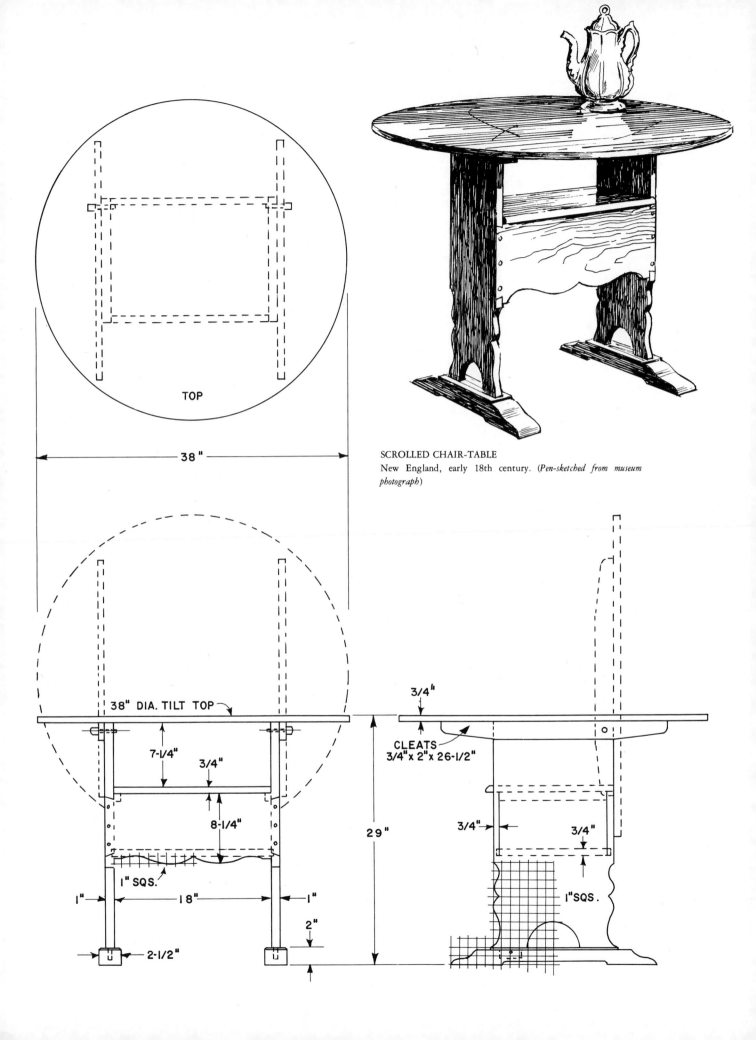

TOP

38 "

SCROLLED CHAIR-TABLE
New England, early 18th century. (*Pen-sketched from museum photograph*)

38" DIA. TILT TOP

7-1/4"

3/4"

8-1/4"

1" SQS.

1"

18"

1"

2-1/2"

2"

29"

3/4"

CLEATS
3/4"x 2"x 26-1/2"

3/4"

3/4"

1"SQS.

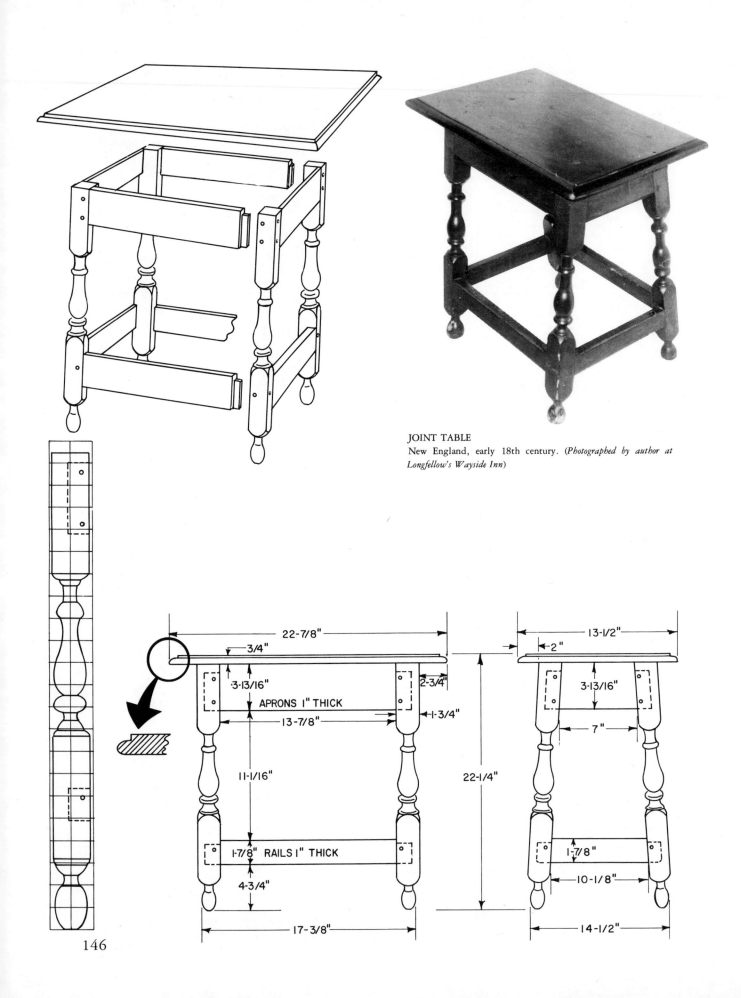

JOINT TABLE
New England, early 18th century. (*Photographed by author at Longfellow's Wayside Inn*)

22-7/8"

3/4"

3·13/16"

APRONS 1" THICK

13-7/8"

2-3/4"

1-3/4"

11-1/16"

22-1/4"

1-7/8" RAILS 1" THICK

4-3/4"

17-3/8"

13-1/2"

2"

3·13/16"

7"

1-7/8"

10-1/8"

14-1/2"

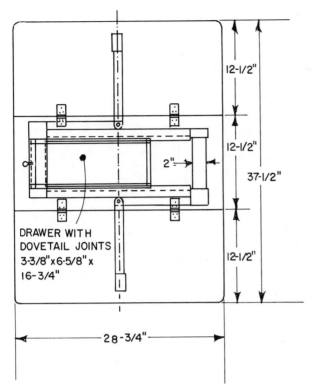

DRAWER WITH
DOVETAIL JOINTS
3-3/8"x6-5/8"x
16-3/4"

12-1/2"

12-1/2"

37-1/2"

12-1/2"

2"

28-3/4"

SPLIT GATE-LEG TABLE
Massachusetts, about 1700. (*Archive photo of museum original*)

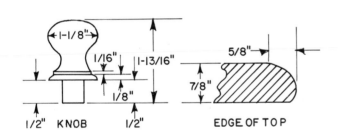

1-1/8"

1/16"

1-13/16"

1/8"

1/2"   KNOB   1/2"

5/8"

7/8"

EDGE OF TOP

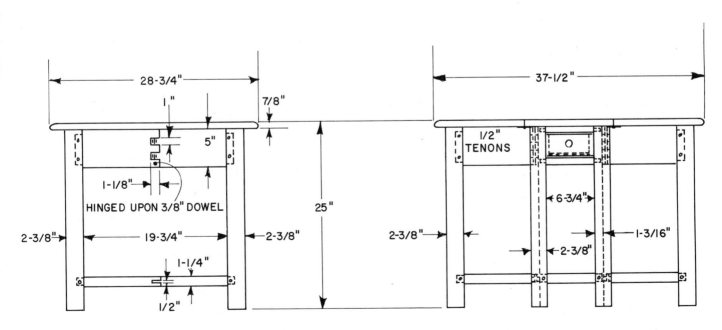

28-3/4"

1"

7/8"

5"

1-1/8"

HINGED UPON 3/8" DOWEL

2-3/8"

19-3/4"

2-3/8"

1-1/4"

1/2"

25"

37-1/2"

1/2"
TENONS

6-3/4"

1-3/16"

2-3/8"

2-3/8"

147

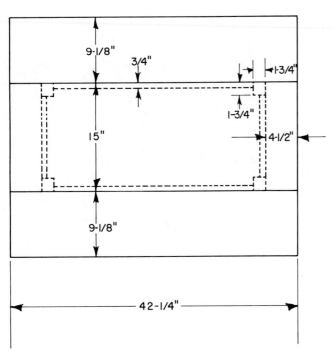

HARVEST TABLE
New England, about 1760. (*Photographed by author at Longfellow's Wayside Inn*)

TOP

TABLE LEAF
RULE HINGED

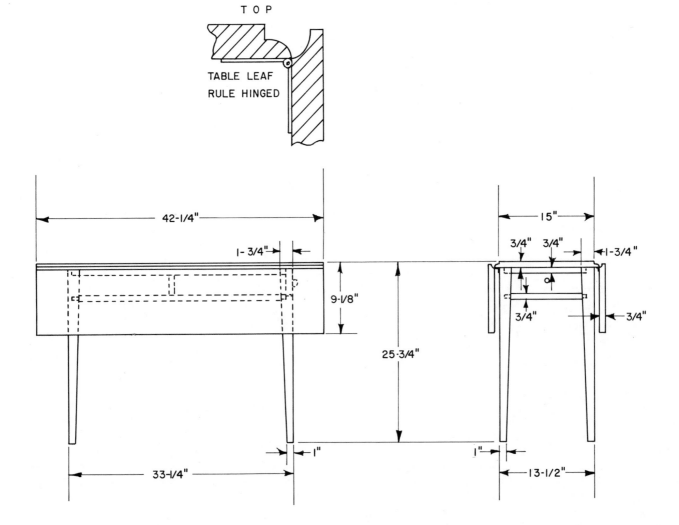

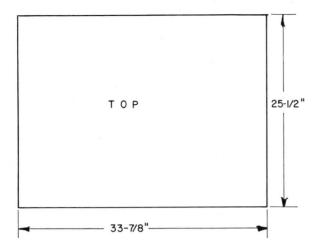

TOP

25-1/2"

33-7/8"

CARVED SPANISH SIDE TABLE
Castile, Spain, about 1790. (*Courtesy, Historic St. Augustine Preservation Board*)

1" SQS.

1/2 PATTERN OF DRAWER FRONT CARVING

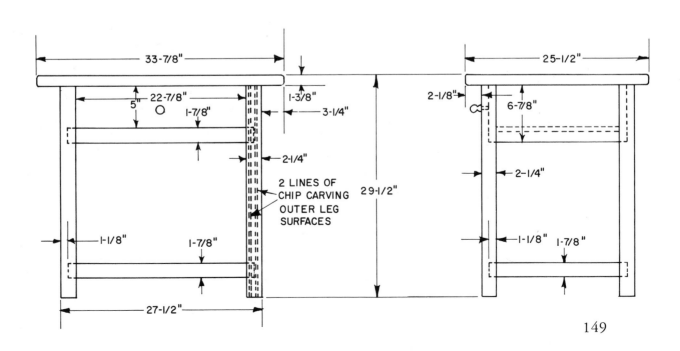

33-7/8"

22-7/8"

5"

1-7/8"

1-3/8"

3-1/4"

2-1/4"

2 LINES OF
CHIP CARVING
OUTER LEG
SURFACES

1-1/8"

1-7/8"

27-1/2"

25-1/2"

2-1/8"

6-7/8"

2-1/4"

29-1/2"

1-1/8" 1-7/8"

149

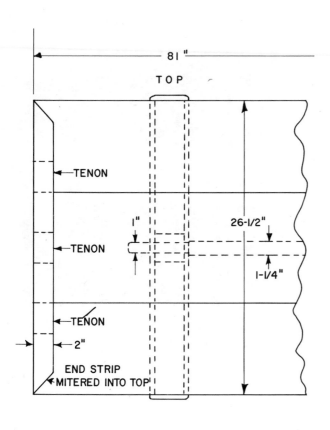

TOP

81"

TENON

TENON

1"

26-1/2"

TENON

1-1/4"

2"

**END STRIP
MITERED INTO TOP**

TRESTLE BOARD ON FRAME
New England, late 17th century. (*Courtesy, American Museum in Britain*)

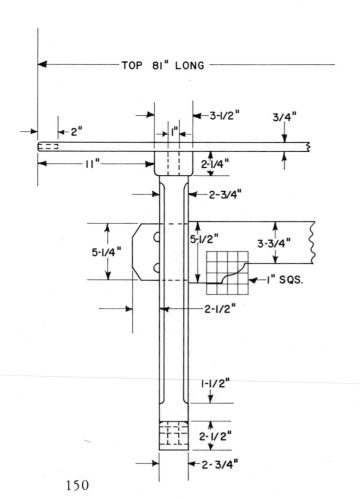

TOP 81" LONG

2"

11"

3-1/2"

1"

3/4"

2-1/4"

2-3/4"

5-1/4"

5-1/2"

3-3/4"

1" SQS.

2-1/2"

1-1/2"

2-1/2"

2-3/4"

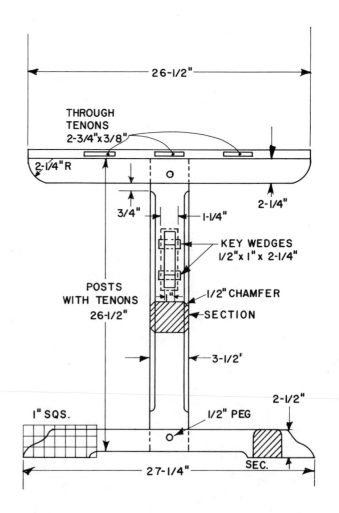

26-1/2"

THROUGH
TENONS
2-3/4"x 3/8"

2-1/4"R

2-1/4"

3/4"

1-1/4"

KEY WEDGES
1/2"x 1"x 2-1/4"

POSTS
WITH TENONS
26-1/2"

1/2" CHAMFER

SECTION

3-1/2"

1" SQS.

1/2" PEG

2-1/2"

27-1/4"

SEC.

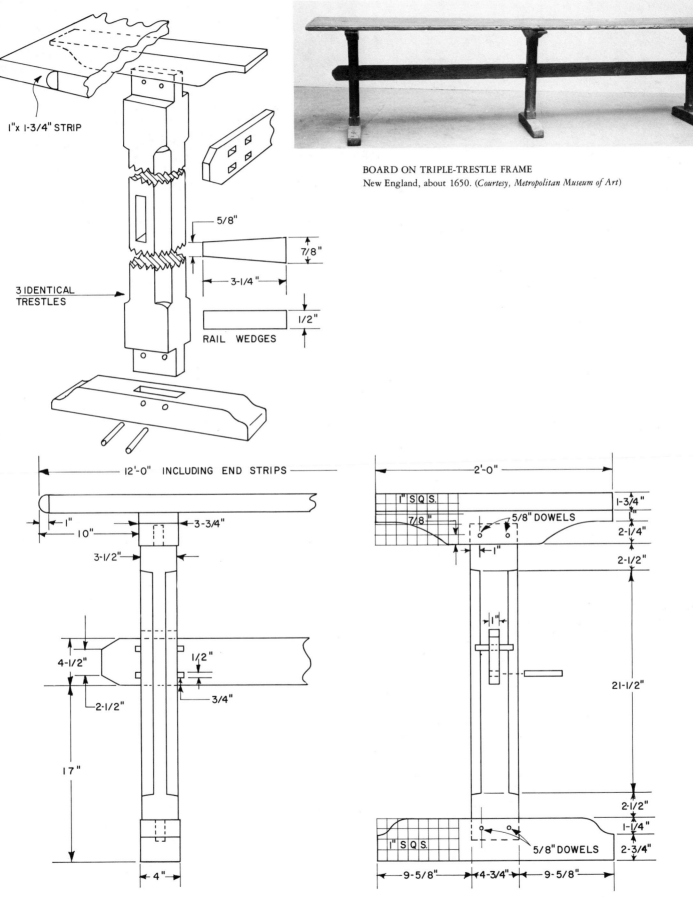

I" x I-3/4" STRIP

BOARD ON TRIPLE-TRESTLE FRAME
New England, about 1650. (*Courtesy, Metropolitan Museum of Art*)

5/8"

7/8"

3-1/4"

3 IDENTICAL
TRESTLES

1/2"

RAIL WEDGES

12'-0" INCLUDING END STRIPS

1"

10"

3-3/4"

3-1/2"

4-1/2"

1/2"

2-1/2"

3/4"

17"

4"

2'-0"

I" SQS.

5/8" DOWELS

1-3/4"

7/8"

2-1/4"

1"

2-1/2"

1"

21-1/2"

2-1/2"

1-1/4"

I" SQS.

5/8" DOWELS

2-3/4"

9-5/8"

4-3/4"

9-5/8"

151

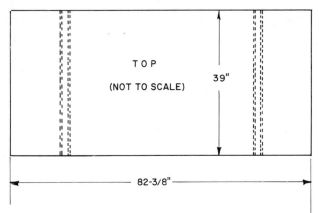

T O P

(NOT TO SCALE)

39"

82-3/8"

SPANISH TRESTLE TABLE
Cataluna, Spain, mid-18th century. (*Courtesy, Historic St. Augustine Preservation Board*)

METAL BRACKET SCROLL
FOOT CURL AND ROSE DETAIL
(2 NEEDED)

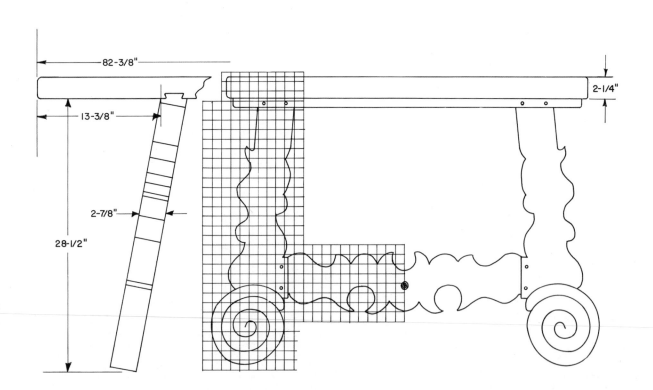

82-3/8"

13-3/8"

2-7/8"

28-1/2"

2-1/4"

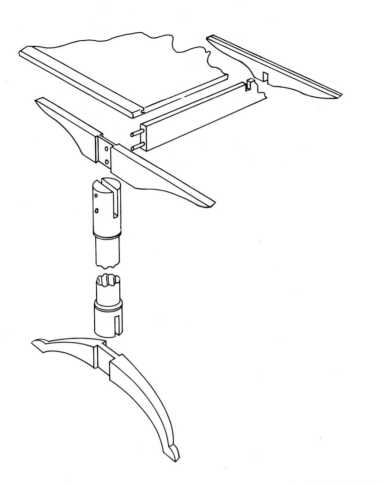

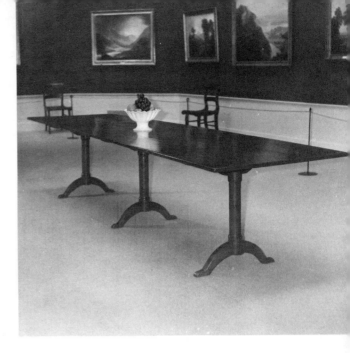

SHAKER TRIPLE-TRESTLE TABLE
New England, about 1840. (*Photographed by author at Fruitlands Museums*)

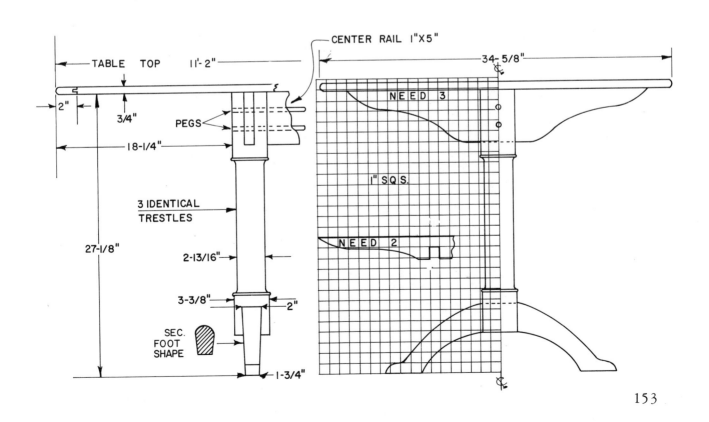

CENTER RAIL 1"X5"

TABLE TOP — 11'- 2"

34-5/8"

NEED 3

2"

3/4"

PEGS

18-1/4"

1" SQS.

3 IDENTICAL TRESTLES

27-1/8"

2-13/16"

NEED 2

3-3/8"   2"

SEC. FOOT SHAPE

1-3/4"

153

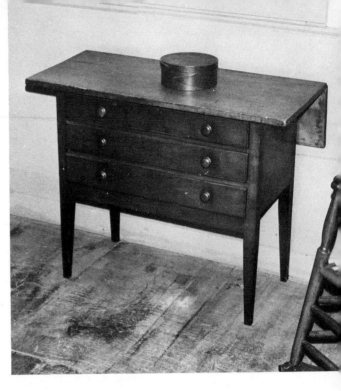

SHAKER SEWING TABLE
Hancock, Massachusetts, about 1850. (*Photographed by author at The Shaker Museum, Old Chatham, New York*)

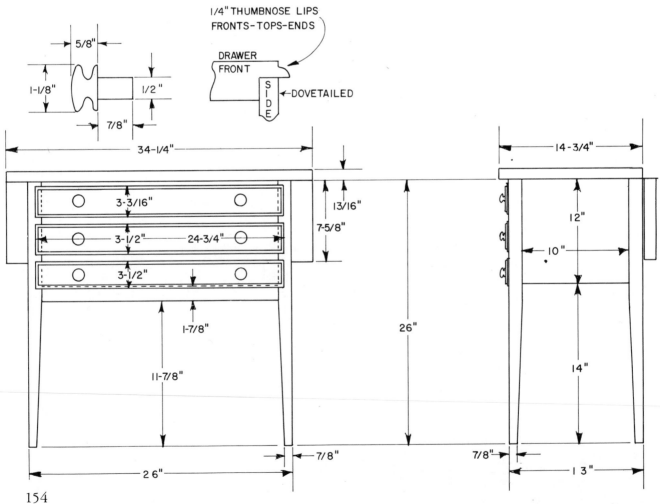

1/4" THUMBNOSE LIPS
FRONTS-TOPS-ENDS

DRAWER
FRONT

S
I
D
E   ←DOVETAILED

5/8"

1-1/8"   1/2"

7/8"

34-1/4"

3-3/16"

3-1/2"   24-3/4"

3-1/2"

13/16"

7-5/8"

1-7/8"

11-7/8"

26"

2 6"   7/8"

14-3/4"

12"

10"

26"

14"

7/8"   7/8"

1 3"

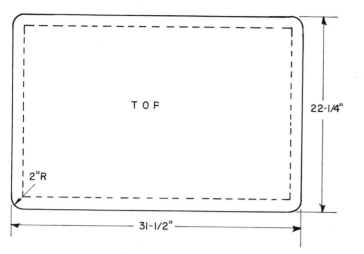

TOP

22-1/4"

2"R

31-1/2"

I"SQS.

LEG TURNING

FRENCH CANADIAN SIDE TABLE

Gentilly, Province of Quebec, late 17th century. (*Photographed by author at The Montreal Museum of Fine Arts*)

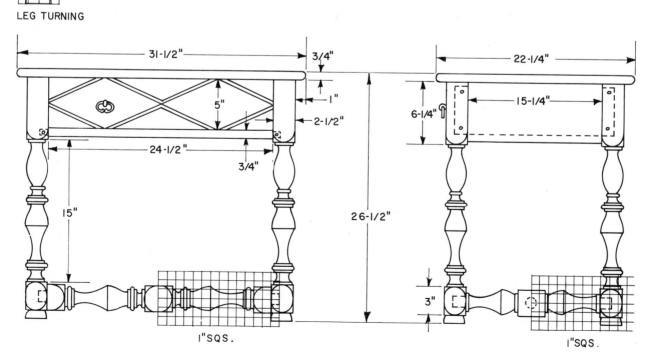

31-1/2"   3/4"

1"

5"

2-1/2"

24-1/2"

3/4"

15"

26-1/2"

22-1/4"

15-1/4"

6-1/4"

3"

I"SQS.

I"SQS.

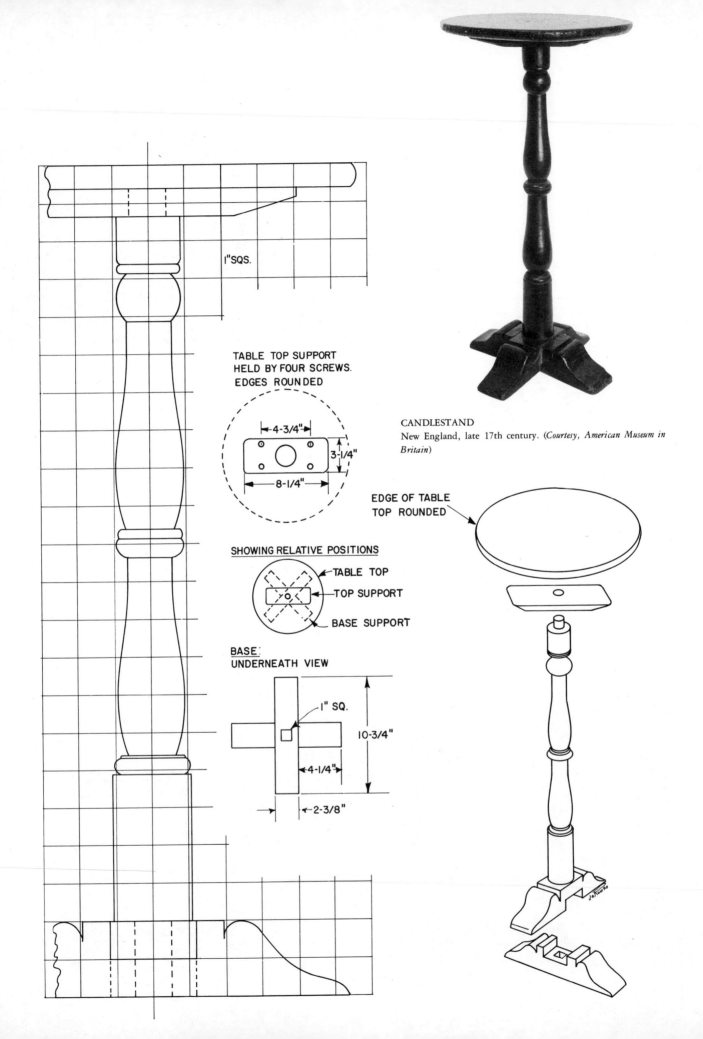

1"SQS.

TABLE TOP SUPPORT
HELD BY FOUR SCREWS.
EDGES ROUNDED

←—4-3/4"—→

3-1/4"

←———8-1/4"———→

SHOWING RELATIVE POSITIONS

TABLE TOP

TOP SUPPORT

BASE SUPPORT

BASE:
UNDERNEATH VIEW

1" SQ.

10-3/4"

←4-1/4"→

←—2-3/8"

CANDLESTAND
New England, late 17th century. (*Courtesy, American Museum in Britain*)

EDGE OF TABLE
TOP ROUNDED

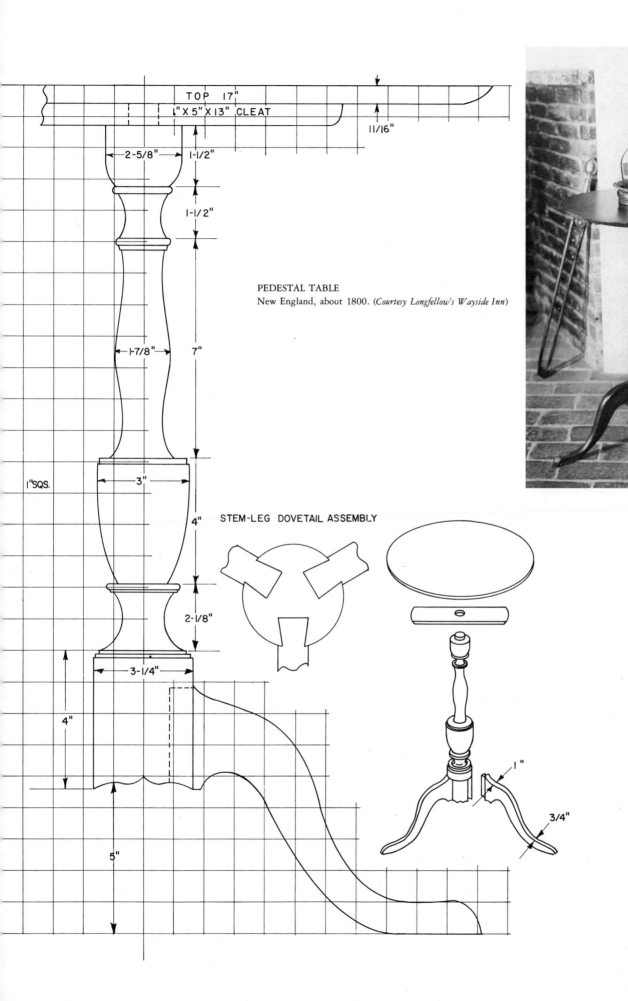

TOP 17"

1"X 5"X13" CLEAT

11/16"

2-5/8" — 1-1/2"

1-1/2"

PEDESTAL TABLE
New England, about 1800. (*Courtesy Longfellow's Wayside Inn*)

1-7/8" — 7"

1"SQS.

3" — 4"

STEM-LEG DOVETAIL ASSEMBLY

2-1/8"

3-1/4"

4"

1"

5"

3/4"

157

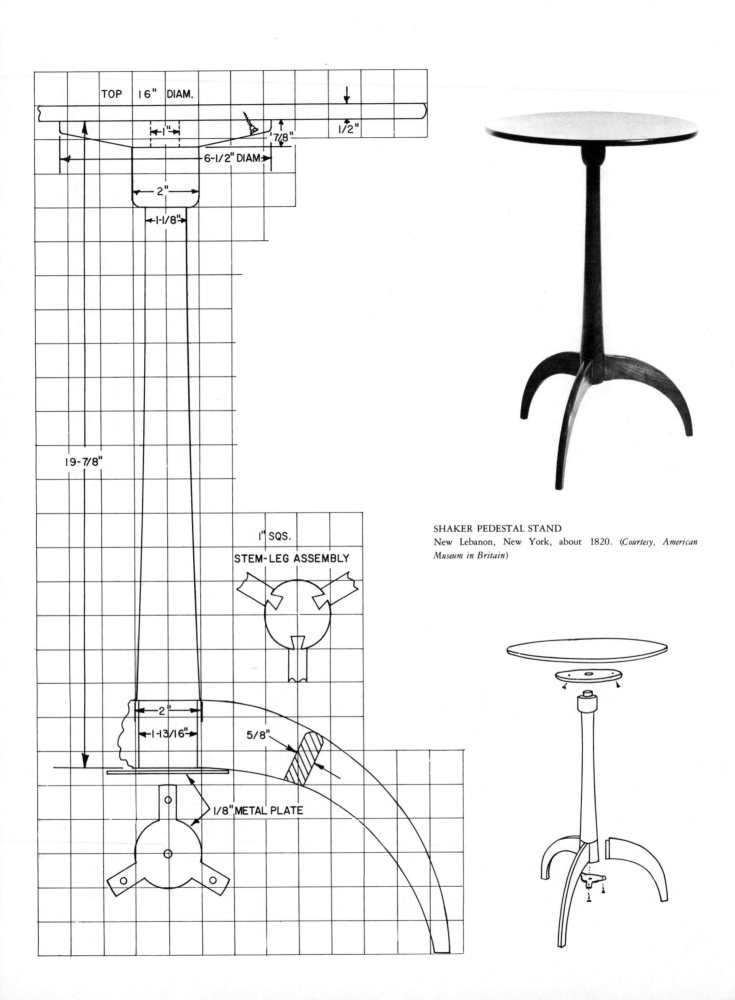

TOP 16" DIAM.

1"

7/8"

1/2"

6-1/2" DIAM.

2"

1-1/8"

19-7/8"

1" SQS.

STEM-LEG ASSEMBLY

2"

1-13/16"

5/8"

1/8" METAL PLATE

SHAKER PEDESTAL STAND
New Lebanon, New York, about 1820. (*Courtesy, American Museum in Britain*)

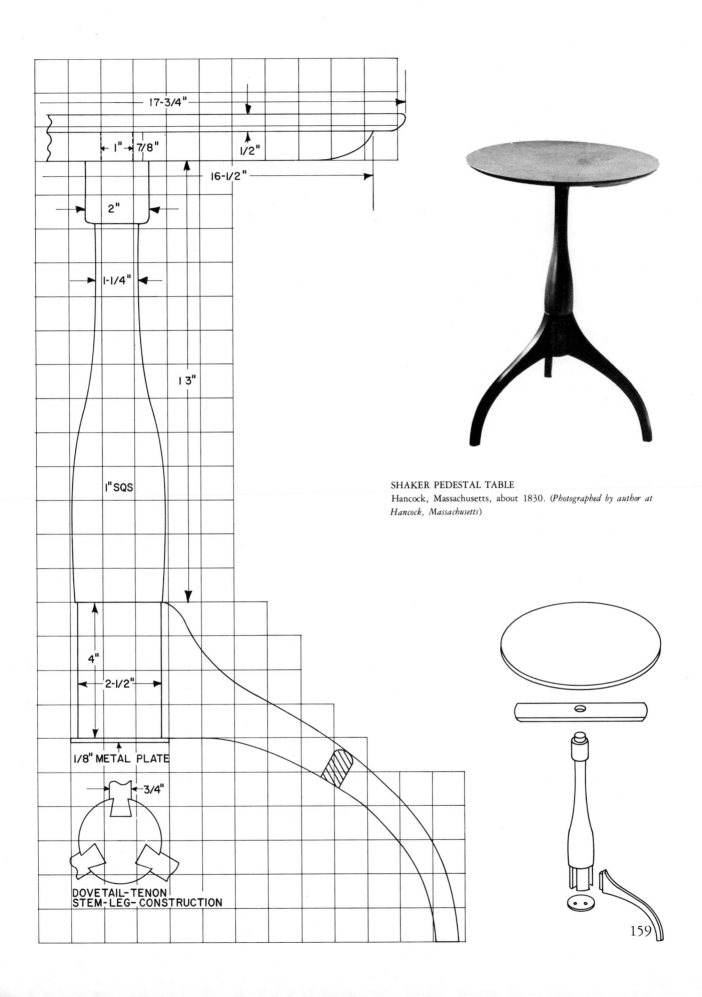

17-3/4"

1" 7/8"

1/2"

16-1/2"

2"

1-1/4"

13"

1"SQS

4"

2-1/2"

1/8" METAL PLATE

3/4"

DOVETAIL-TENON
STEM-LEG-CONSTRUCTION

SHAKER PEDESTAL TABLE

Hancock, Massachusetts, about 1830. (*Photographed by author at Hancock, Massachusetts*)

159

SHAKER SORTING STAND
New Lebanon, New York, about 1840. (*Photographed by author at Hancock, Massachusetts*)

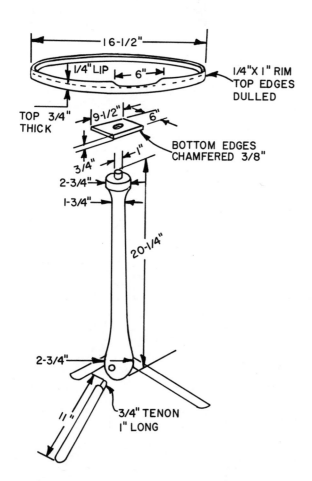

16-1/2"

1/4" LIP

6"

1/4" X 1" RIM
TOP EDGES
DULLED

TOP 3/4"
THICK

9-1/2"

6"

BOTTOM EDGES
CHAMFERED 3/8"

3/4"

1"

2-3/4"

1-3/4"

20-1/4"

2-3/4"

11"

3/4" TENON
1" LONG

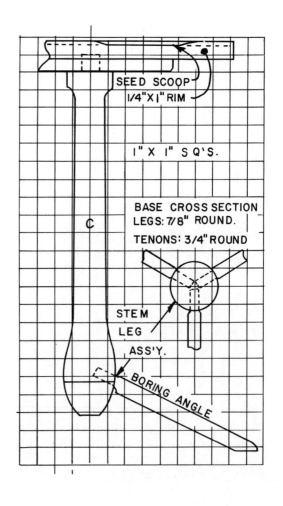

SEED SCOOP
1/4" X 1" RIM

1" X 1" SQ'S.

C

BASE CROSS SECTION
LEGS: 7/8" ROUND.
TENONS: 3/4" ROUND

STEM
LEG
ASS'Y.

BORING ANGLE

160

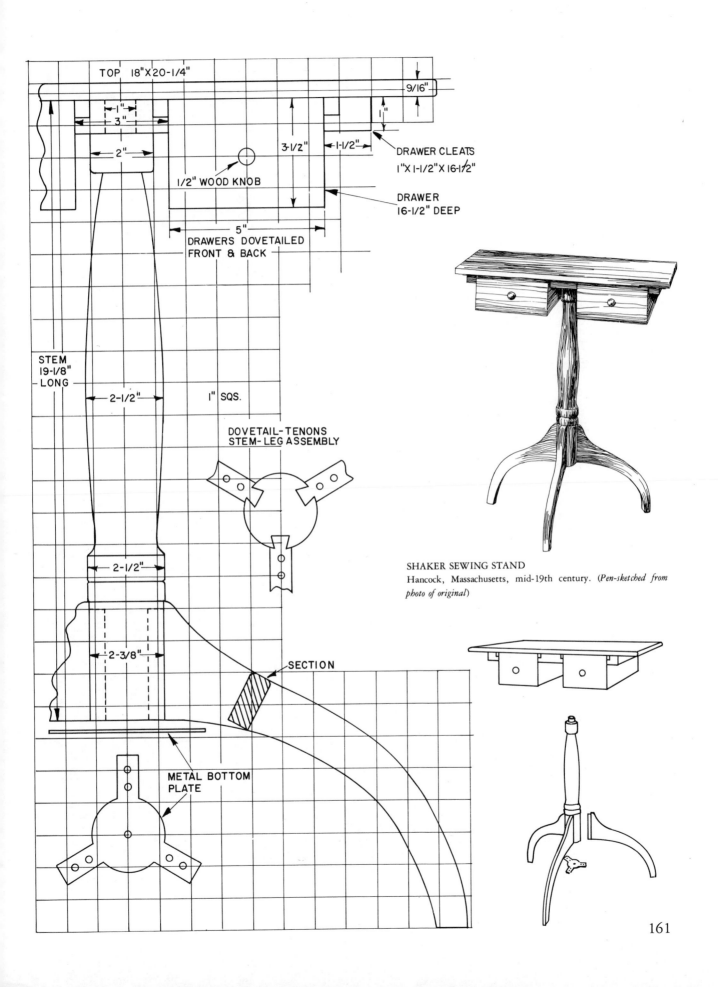

TOP 18"X20-1/4"

9/16"

1"
3"

2"

1/2" WOOD KNOB

3-1/2"

1-1/2"

DRAWER CLEATS
1"X 1-1/2"X 16-1/2"

1"

DRAWER
16-1/2" DEEP

5"

DRAWERS DOVETAILED
FRONT & BACK

STEM
19-1/8"
LONG

2-1/2"

1" SQS.

DOVETAIL-TENONS
STEM-LEG ASSEMBLY

2-1/2"

2-3/8"

SECTION

METAL BOTTOM
PLATE

SHAKER SEWING STAND
Hancock, Massachusetts, mid-19th century. (*Pen-sketched from photo of original*)

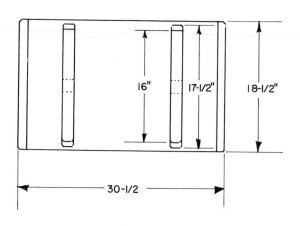

16" 17-1/2" 18-1/2"

30-1/2

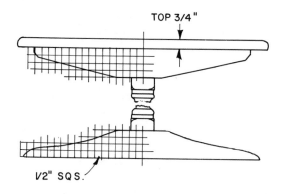

TOP 3/4"

1/2" SQS.

TRESTLE TAVERN TABLE
Connecticut, about 1670–1690. (*Reproduced from original in the Wadsworth Atheneum*)

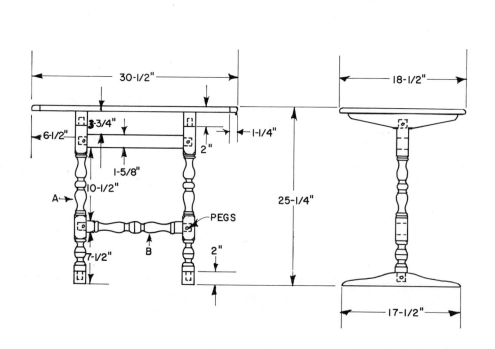

30-1/2"

3-3/4"

6-1/2"

1-1/4"

2"

1-5/8"

10-1/2"

A→

PEGS

B

7-1/2"

2"

18-1/2"

25-1/4"

17-1/2"

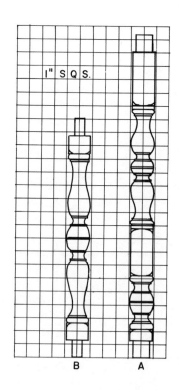

1" SQS.

B   A

162

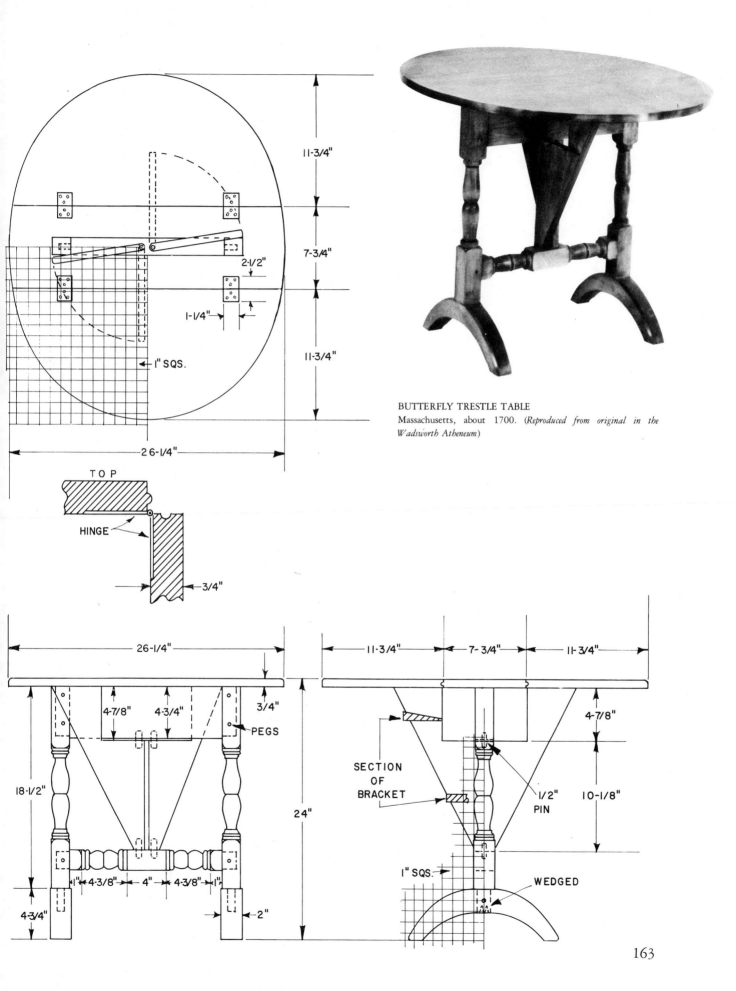

11-3/4"

7-3/4"

2-1/2"

1-1/4"

11-3/4"

1" SQS.

26-1/4"

TOP

HINGE

3/4"

BUTTERFLY TRESTLE TABLE
Massachusetts, about 1700. (*Reproduced from original in the Wadsworth Atheneum*)

26-1/4"

4-7/8" 4-3/4"

3/4"

PEGS

18-1/2"

24"

1" 4-3/8" 4" 4-3/8" 1"

4-3/4"

2"

11-3/4" 7-3/4" 11-3/4"

4-7/8"

SECTION
OF
BRACKET

1/2"
PIN

10-1/8"

1" SQS.

WEDGED

163

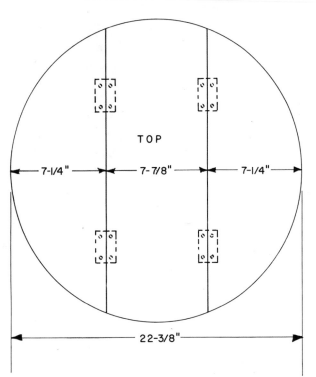

TOP

7-1/4"　　7-7/8"　　7-1/4"

22-3/8"

SMALL BUTTERFLY TABLE
New England, about 1700. (*Courtesy, Longfellow's Wayside Inn*)

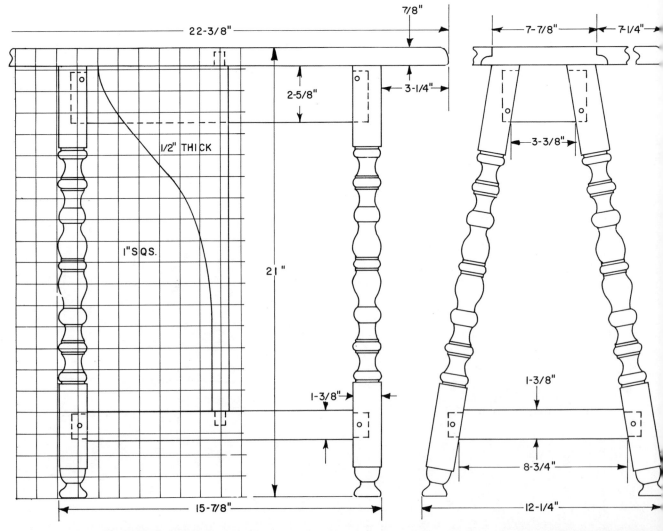

22-3/8"

7/8"

7-7/8"　　7-1/4"

2-5/8"

3-1/4"

1/2" THICK

3-3/8"

1" SQS.

21"

1-3/8"

1-3/8"

15-7/8"

8-3/4"

12-1/4"

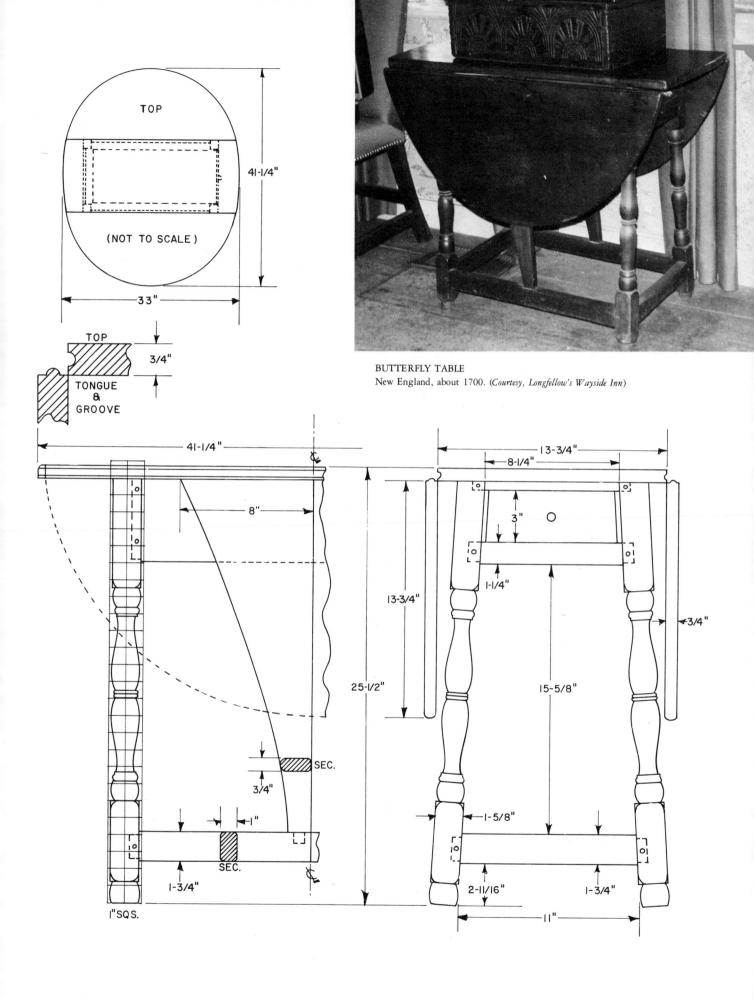

TOP

41-1/4"

(NOT TO SCALE)

33"

TOP

3/4"

TONGUE
&
GROOVE

BUTTERFLY TABLE
New England, about 1700. (*Courtesy, Longfellow's Wayside Inn*)

41-1/4"

8"

25-1/2"

SEC.

3/4"

1"

SEC.

1-3/4"

1"SQS.

13-3/4"

8-1/4"

3"

1-1/4"

13-3/4"

3/4"

15-5/8"

1-5/8"

2-11/16"

1-3/4"

11"

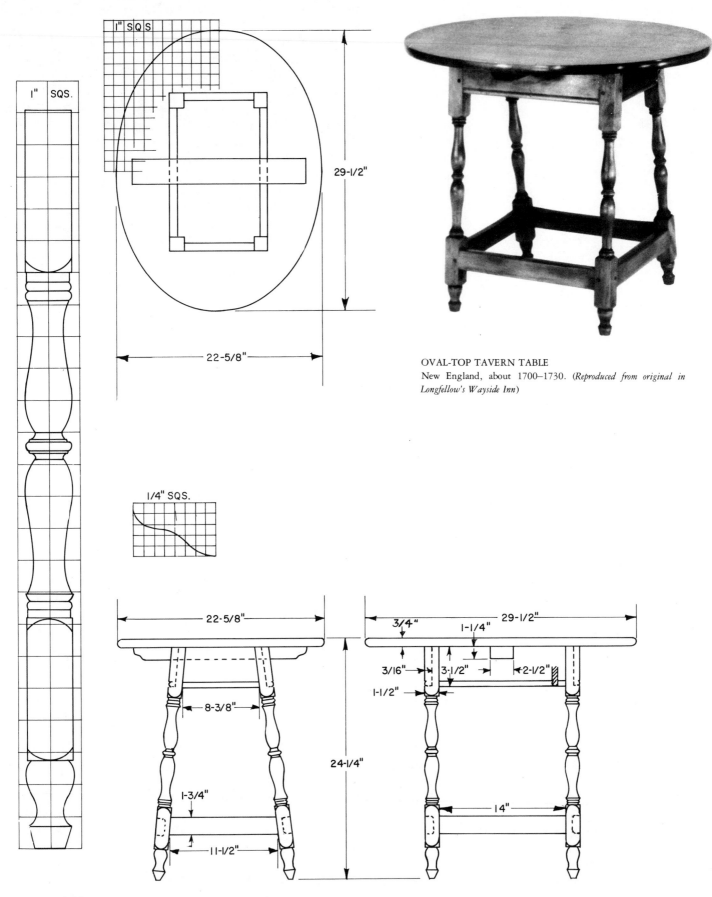

1" SQS.

1" SQS

29-1/2"

22-5/8"

1/4" SQS.

OVAL-TOP TAVERN TABLE
New England, about 1700–1730. (*Reproduced from original in Longfellow's Wayside Inn*)

22-5/8"

8-3/8"

1-3/4"

11-1/2"

24-1/4"

3/4"

1-1/4"

29-1/2"

3/16"

3-1/2"

2-1/2"

1-1/2"

14"

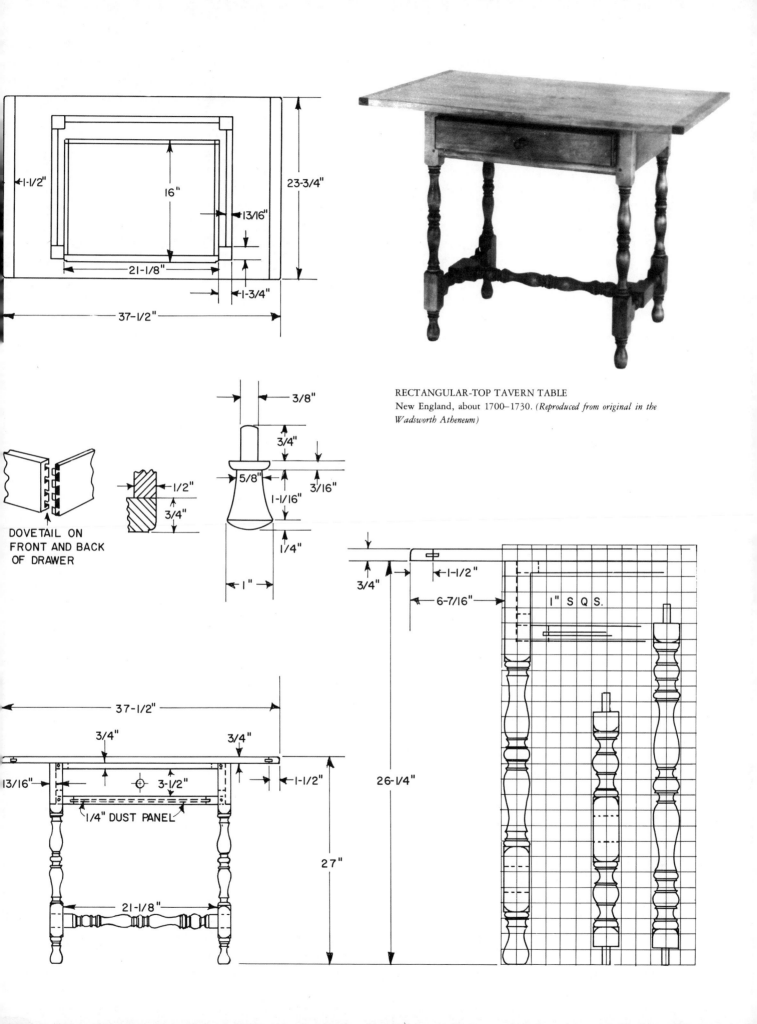

1-1/2" · **16"** · **23-3/4"** · **13/16"** · **21-1/8"** · **1-3/4"** · **37-1/2"**

RECTANGULAR-TOP TAVERN TABLE
New England, about 1700–1730. *(Reproduced from original in the Wadsworth Atheneum)*

DOVETAIL ON FRONT AND BACK OF DRAWER

1/2" · **3/4"** · **3/8"** · **3/4"** · **5/8"** · **3/16"** · **1-1/16"** · **1/4"** · **1"**

3/4" · **1-1/2"** · **6-7/16"** · **1" SQS.**

37-1/2" · **3/4"** · **3/4"** · **13/16"** · **3-1/2"** · **1-1/2"** · **1/4" DUST PANEL** · **26-1/4"** · **27"** · **21-1/8"**

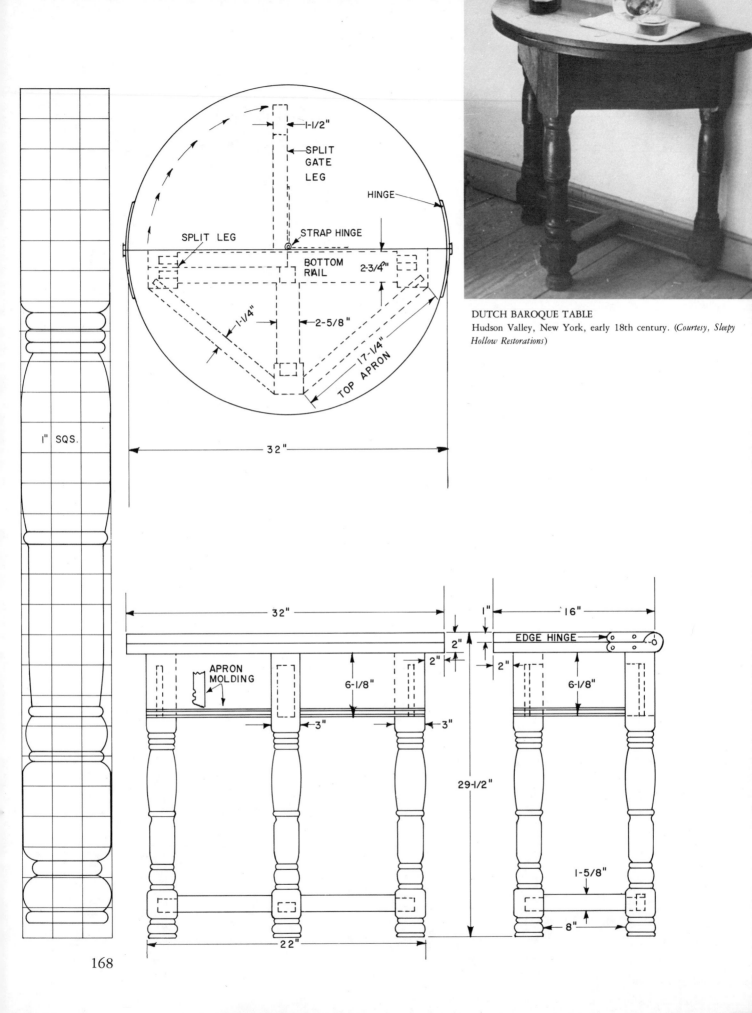

1-1/2"

SPLIT
GATE
LEG

HINGE

SPLIT LEG

STRAP HINGE

BOTTOM
RAIL

2-3/4"

1-1/4"

2-5/8"

17-1/4"

TOP APRON

1" SQS.

32"

DUTCH BAROQUE TABLE
Hudson Valley, New York, early 18th century. (*Courtesy, Sleepy Hollow Restorations*)

32"

1"

16"

EDGE HINGE

2"

2"

2"

APRON
MOLDING

6-1/8"

6-1/8"

3"

3"

29-1/2"

1-5/8"

8"

22"

168

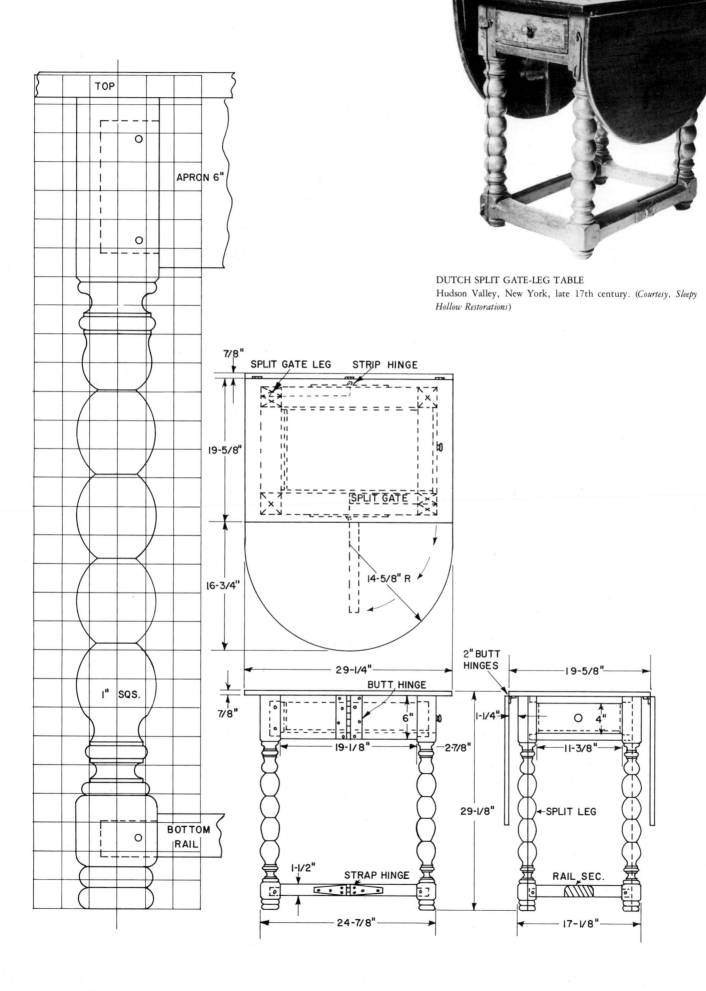

TOP

APRON 6"

DUTCH SPLIT GATE-LEG TABLE
Hudson Valley, New York, late 17th century. (*Courtesy, Sleepy Hollow Restorations*)

1" SQS.

BOTTOM RAIL

7/8"

SPLIT GATE LEG   STRIP HINGE

19-5/8"

SPLIT GATE

16-3/4"

14-5/8" R

29-1/4"

BUTT HINGE

7/8"

6"

19-1/8"   2-7/8"

1-1/2"   STRAP HINGE

24-7/8"

2" BUTT HINGES

19-5/8"

1-1/4"   4"

11-3/8"

SPLIT LEG

29-1/8"

RAIL SEC.

17-1/8"

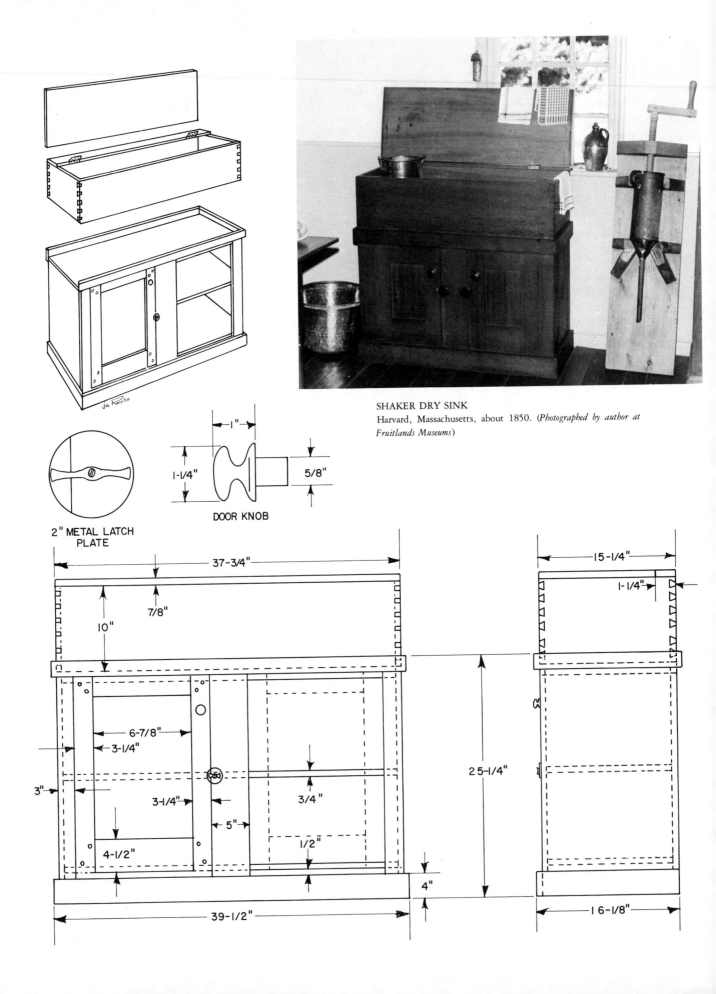

SHAKER DRY SINK

Harvard, Massachusetts, about 1850. (*Photographed by author at Fruitlands Museums*)

DOOR KNOB

2" METAL LATCH PLATE

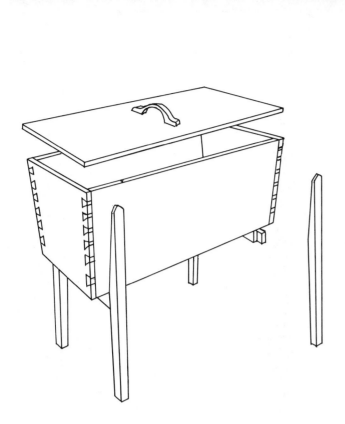

DOUGH BOX
Hudson Valley, New York, about 1800. (*Courtesy, Sleepy Hollow Restorations*)

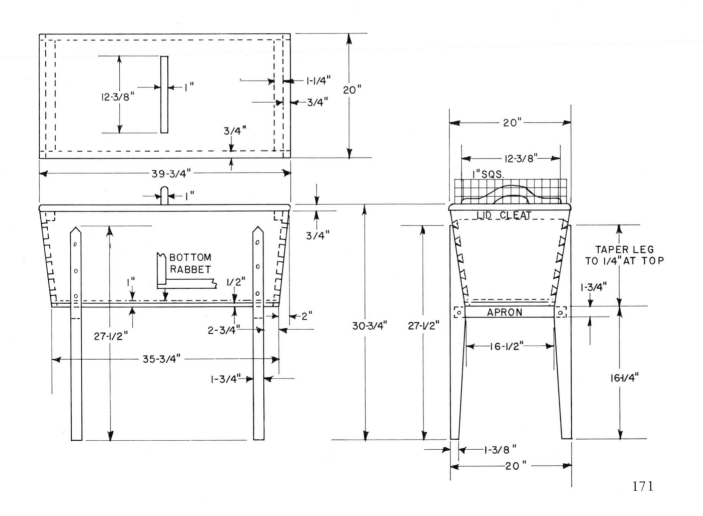

12-3/8" 1" 1-1/4" 20" 3/4" 3/4" 39-3/4"

1"

BOTTOM RABBET 1" 1/2"

3/4"

27-1/2" 2-3/4" 2" 35-3/4" 1-3/4" 30-3/4"

1"SQS. 20" 12-3/8"

LID CLEAT

TAPER LEG TO 1/4" AT TOP

APRON 1-3/4"

27-1/2" 16-1/2" 16-1/4"

1-3/8" 20"

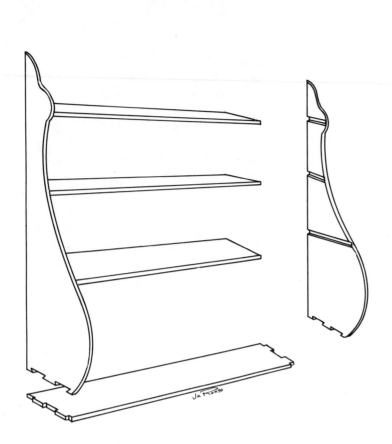

PINE SET OF SHELVES
New England, late 18th century. (*Courtesy, Longfellow's Wayside Inn*)

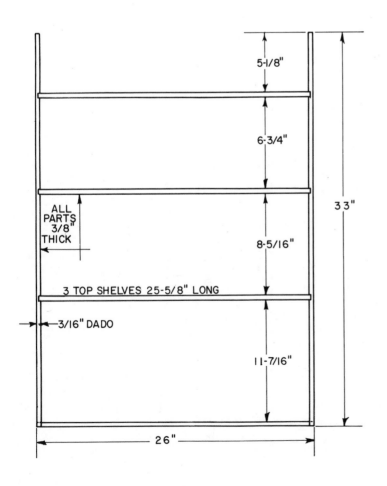

ALL PARTS 3/8" THICK

5-1/8"

6-3/4"

8-5/16"

33"

3 TOP SHELVES 25-5/8" LONG

3/16" DADO

11-7/16"

26"

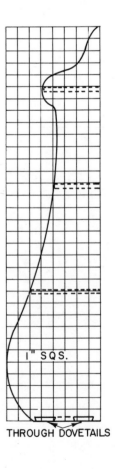

1" SQS.

THROUGH DOVETAILS

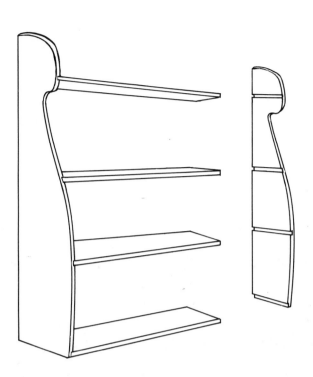

HANGING SHELVES
New England, about 1825. (*Photographed by author at Fruitlands Museums*)

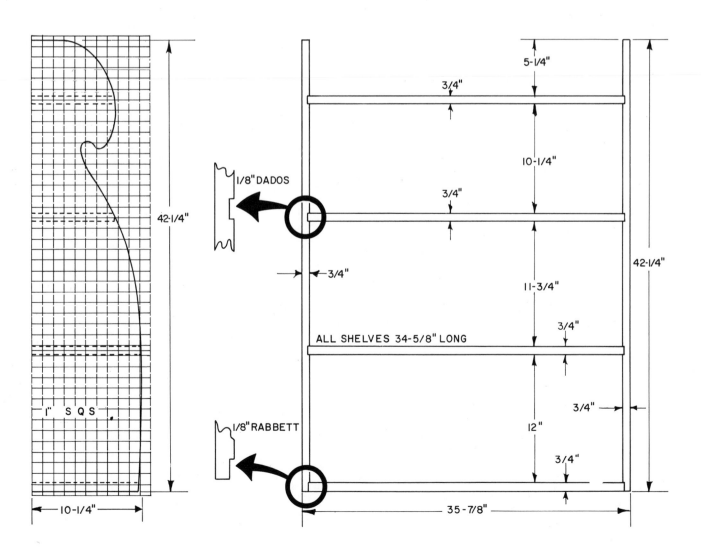

42-1/4"

10-1/4"

1" S Q S

1/8" DADOS

1/8" RABBETT

5-1/4"

3/4"

10-1/4"

3/4"

3/4"

11-3/4"

ALL SHELVES 34-5/8" LONG

3/4"

42-1/4"

3/4"

12"

3/4"

35-7/8"

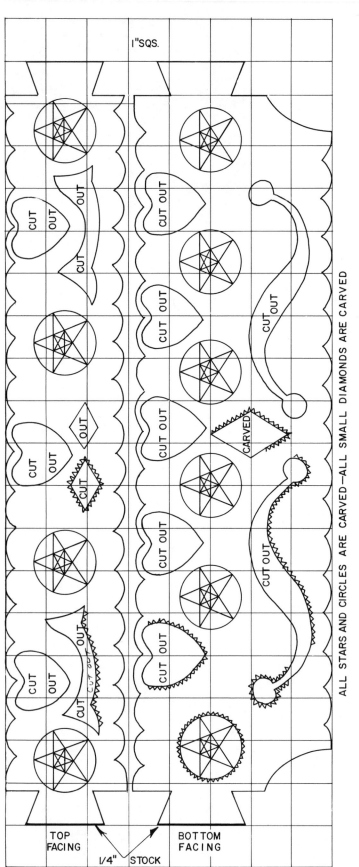

1"SQS.

CUT OUT
CUT OUT
CUT OUT
CUT OUT
CUT OUT
CUT OUT
CUT OUT
CUT OUT
CUT OUT
CUT OUT
CUT OUT
CUT OUT
CUT OUT
CUT OUT
CUT
OUT
CARVED

ALL STARS AND CIRCLES ARE CARVED—ALL SMALL DIAMONDS ARE CARVED

TOP FACING

BOTTOM FACING

1/4" STOCK

PENNSYLVANIA GERMAN PLATE RACK
Pennsylvania, early 19th century. (*Courtesy, American Museum in Britain*)

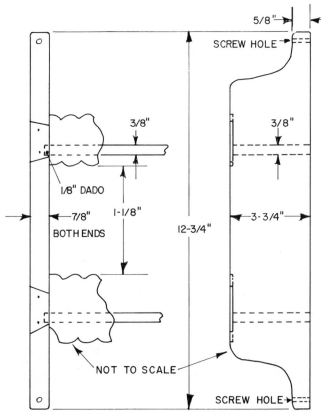

5/8"

SCREW HOLE

3/8"

1/8" DADO

3/8"

7/8"

BOTH ENDS

1-1/8"

12-3/4"

3-3/4"

NOT TO SCALE

SCREW HOLE

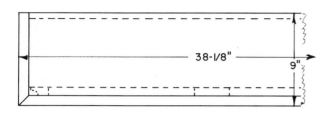

METAL LOCK PLATE

38-1/8"

9"

PENNSYLVANIA GERMAN HANGING CUPBOARD
Pennsylvania, late 18th century. (*Courtesy, American Museum in Britain*)

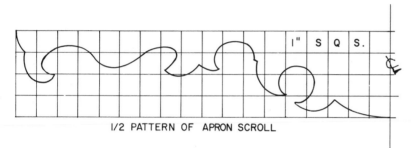

1" S Q S.

1/2 PATTERN OF APRON SCROLL

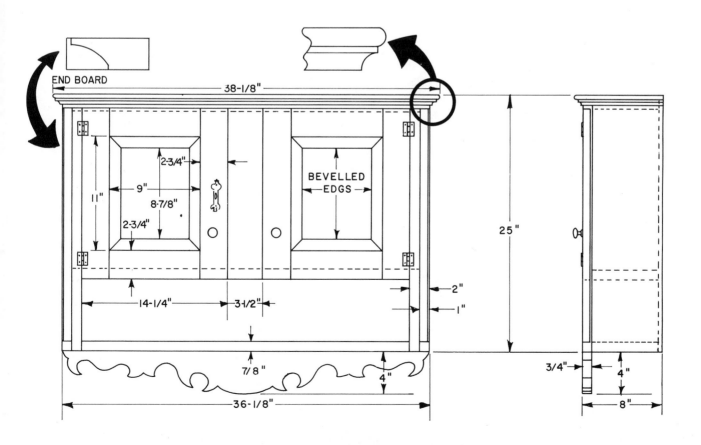

END BOARD

38-1/8"

2-3/4"

9"

11"

8-7/8"

2-3/4"

BEVELLED EDGS

25"

14-1/4"

3-1/2"

2"

1"

7/8"

4"

36-1/8"

3/4"

4"

8"

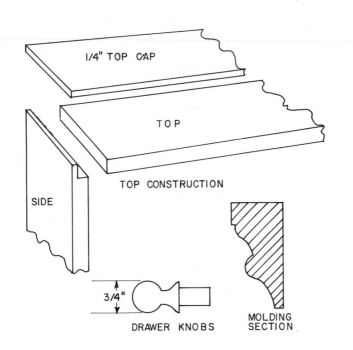

1/4" TOP CAP

TOP

TOP CONSTRUCTION

SIDE

3/4"

DRAWER KNOBS

MOLDING SECTION

HANGING SHELVES
New England, late 18th century. (*Photographed by author at Sleepy Hollow Restorations*)

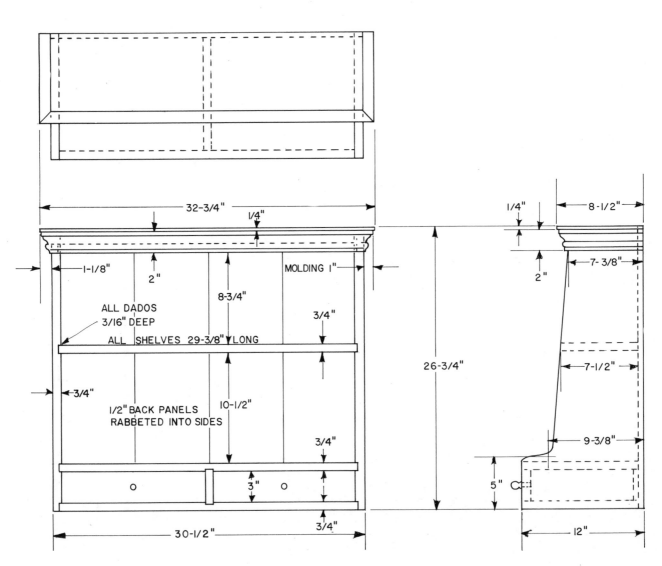

32-3/4"

1/4"

1-1/8"

2"

MOLDING 1"

8-3/4"

3/4"

ALL DADOS
3/16" DEEP

ALL SHELVES 29-3/8" LONG

3/4"

1/2" BACK PANELS
RABBETED INTO SIDES

10-1/2"

3/4"

3"

30-1/2"

3/4"

1/4"

8-1/2"

7-3/8"

2"

26-3/4"

7-1/2"

9-3/8"

5"

12"

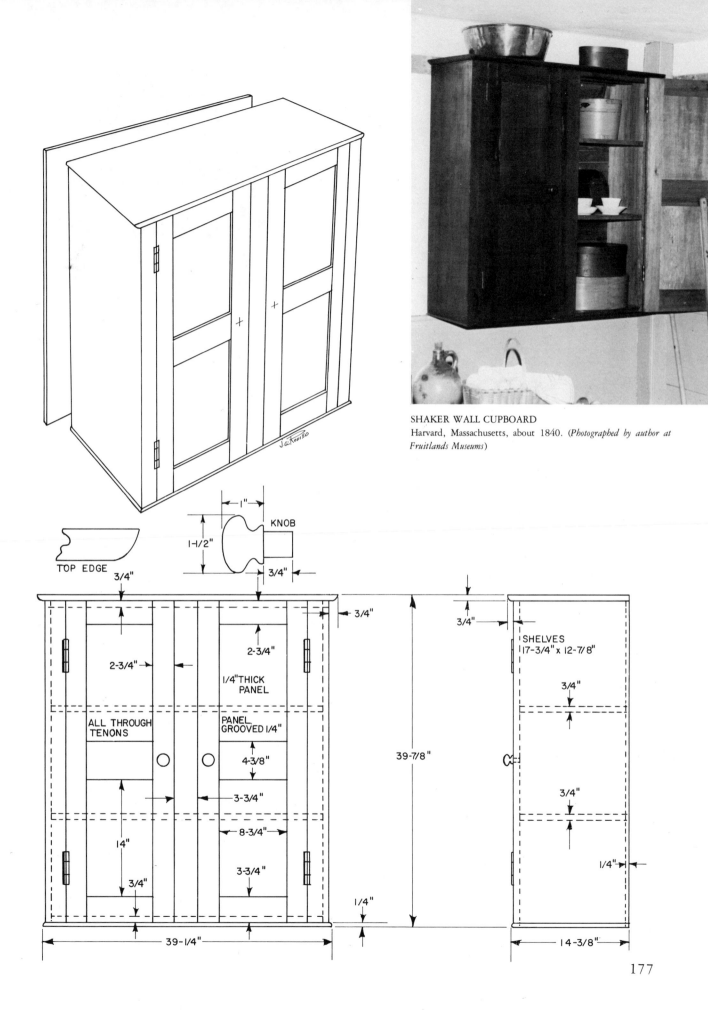

SHAKER WALL CUPBOARD
Harvard, Massachusetts, about 1840. (*Photographed by author at Fruitlands Museums*)

TOP EDGE

KNOB

1"

1-1/2"

3/4"

3/4"

3/4"

3/4"

SHELVES
17-3/4" x 12-7/8"

2-3/4"

2-3/4"

1/4" THICK
PANEL

3/4"

ALL THROUGH
TENONS

PANEL
GROOVED 1/4"

4-3/8"

3-3/4"

3/4"

39-7/8"

3/4"

14"

8-3/4"

3/4"

3-3/4"

1/4"

1/4"

39-1/4"

14-3/8"

177

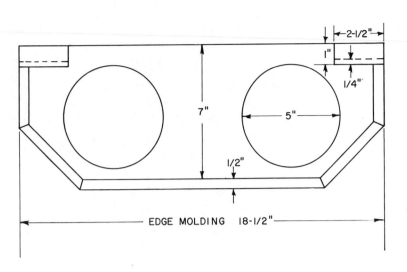

EDGE MOLDING 18-1/2"

2-1/2"

1"

1/4"

7"

5"

1/2"

SPANISH PITCHER RACK

Santilla del Mar, Spain, about 1800. (*Courtesy, Historic St. Augustine Preservation Board*)

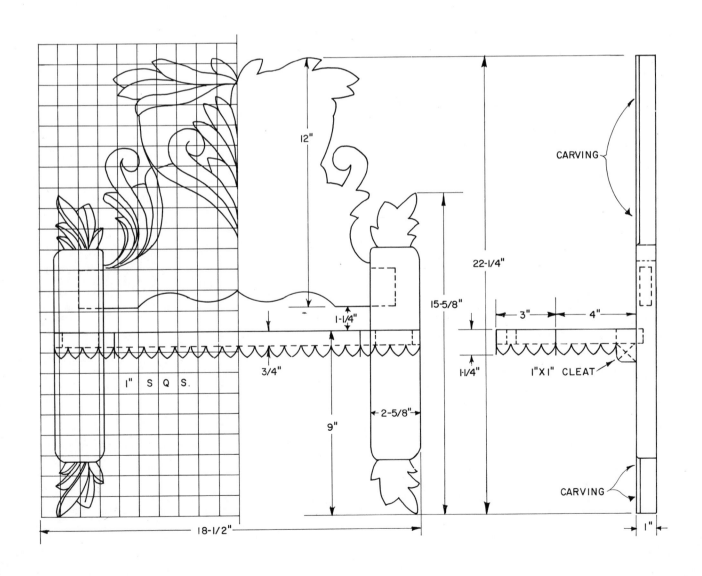

12"

22-1/4"

CARVING

15-5/8"

1-1/4"

3/4"

3"

4"

1-1/4"

1" S Q S.

2-5/8"

9"

1"X1" CLEAT

CARVING

18-1/2"

1"

WALL BOX

Hudson Valley, New York, 18th century. (*Photographed by author at Sleepy Hollow Restorations*)

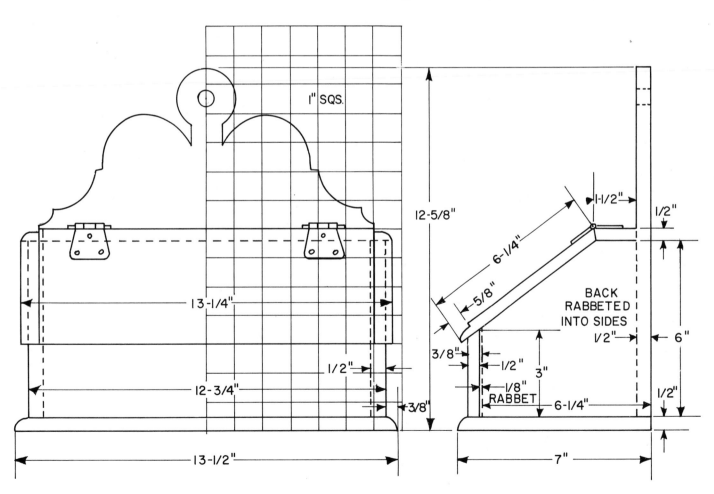

1" SQS.

12-5/8"

13-1/4"

13-3/4" → 12-3/4"

1/2"

3/8"

13-1/2"

6-1/4"

5/8"

1-1/2"

1/2"

BACK RABBETED INTO SIDES

1/2"

6"

3/8"

1/2"

3"

1/8" RABBET

6-1/4"

1/2"

7"

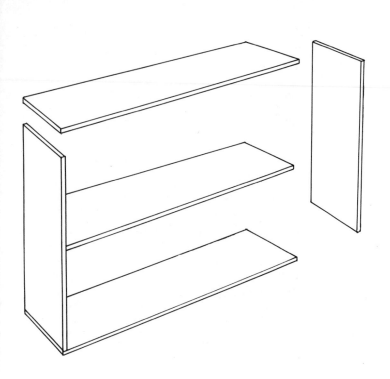

THOREAU'S BOOKCASES
Built of driftwood by Henry David Thoreau in 1855. (*Photographed by author at Fruitlands Museums*)

1/2" SQS.

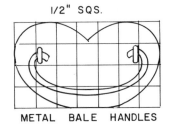

METAL BALE HANDLES

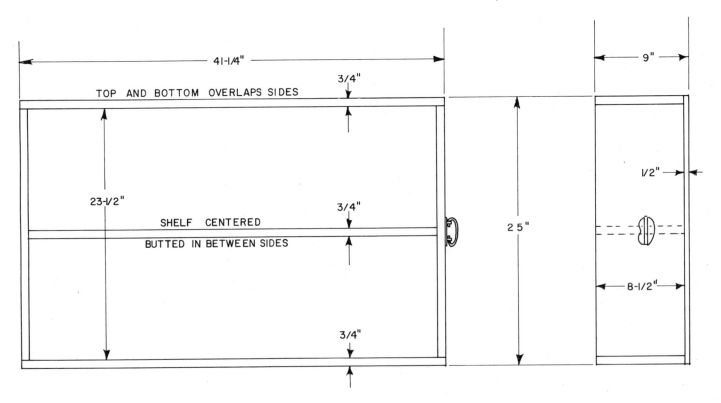

41-1/4"

3/4"

9"

TOP AND BOTTOM OVERLAPS SIDES

23-1/2"

1/2"

3/4"

SHELF CENTERED

25"

BUTTED IN BETWEEN SIDES

8-1/2"

3/4"

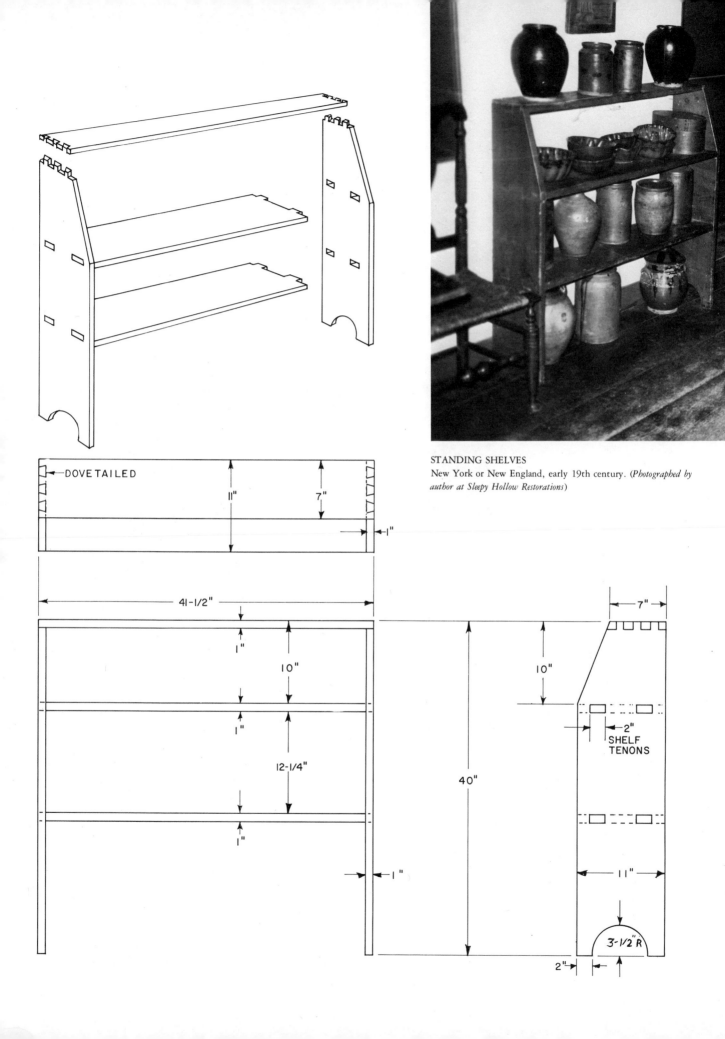

STANDING SHELVES
New York or New England, early 19th century. (*Photographed by author at Sleepy Hollow Restorations*)

DOVETAILED

11"

7"

1"

41-1/2"

1"

10"

1"

12-1/4"

1"

1"

40"

7"

10"

2"
SHELF
TENONS

11"

3-1/2"R

2"

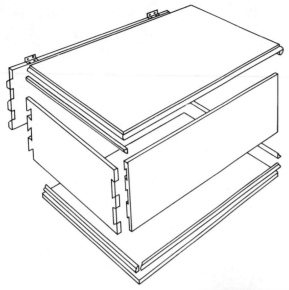

CARVED BIBLE BOX
New England, about 1680–1700. (*Courtesy, Longfellow's Wayside Inn*)

TOP THUMBNOSE EDGE
END STRIP

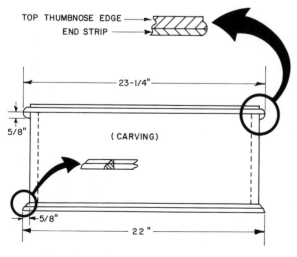

(CARVING)

23-1/4"

5/8"

5/8"

22"

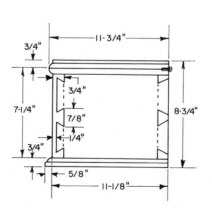

11-3/4"

3/4"

3/4"

7/8"

7-1/4"

1/4"

3/4"

8-3/4"

5/8"

11-1/8"

182

TYPICAL CARVED PATTERNS

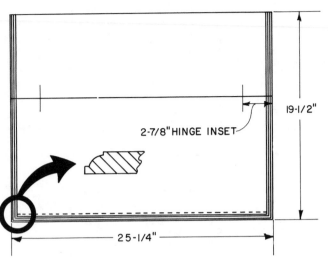

2-7/8" HINGE INSET

19-1/2"

25-1/4"

CARVED DESK BOX
New England (possibly England), late 17th century. (*Photographed by author at Fruitlands Museums*)

WROUGHT IRON HINGE & HASP

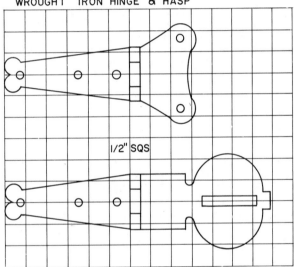

1/2" SQS

CORNER CONSTRUCTION

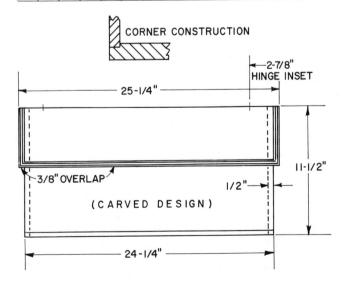

2-7/8" HINGE INSET

25-1/4"

3/8" OVERLAP

1/2"

(CARVED DESIGN)

11-1/2"

24-1/4"

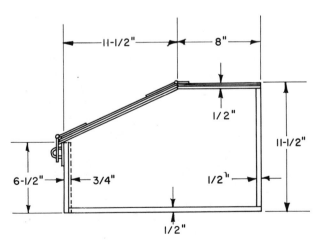

11-1/2"   8"

1/2"

11-1/2"

6-1/2"   3/4"   1/2"

1/2"

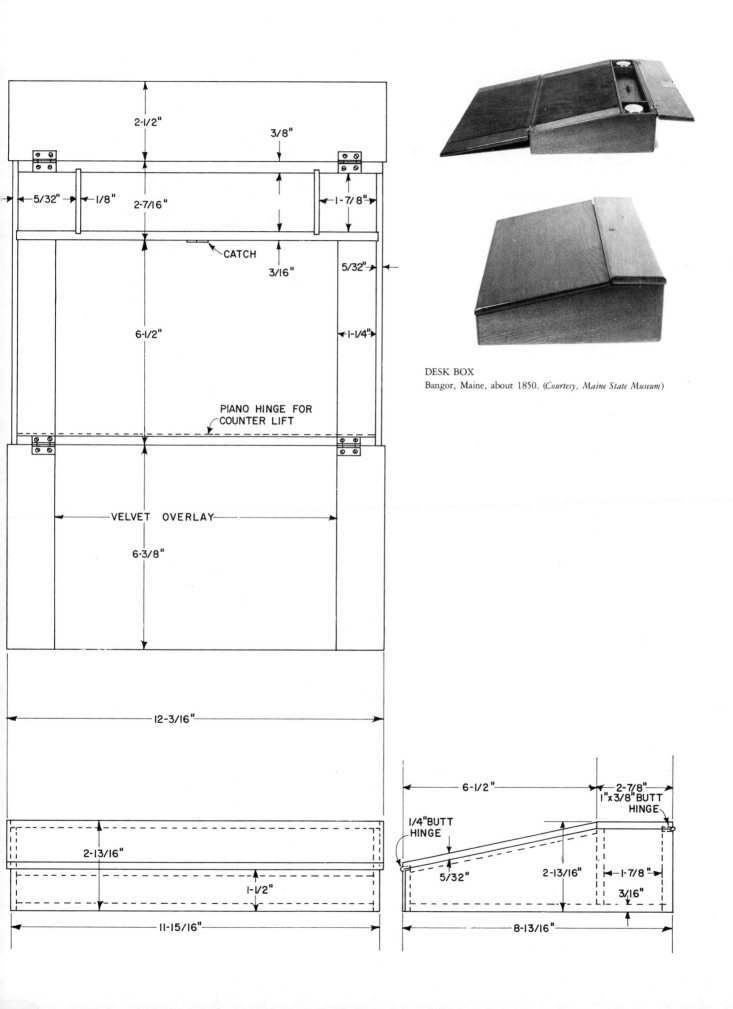

2-1/2"

3/8"

5/32" | 1/8" | 2-7/16" | 1-7/8"

CATCH

3/16" | 5/32"

6-1/2" | 1-1/4"

PIANO HINGE FOR COUNTER LIFT

VELVET OVERLAY

6-3/8"

12-3/16"

2-13/16"

1-1/2"

11-15/16"

6-1/2" | 2-7/8"

1"x3/8"BUTT HINGE

1/4"BUTT HINGE

5/32" | 2-13/16" | 1-7/8"

3/16"

8-13/16"

DESK BOX
Bangor, Maine, about 1850. (*Courtesy, Maine State Museum*)

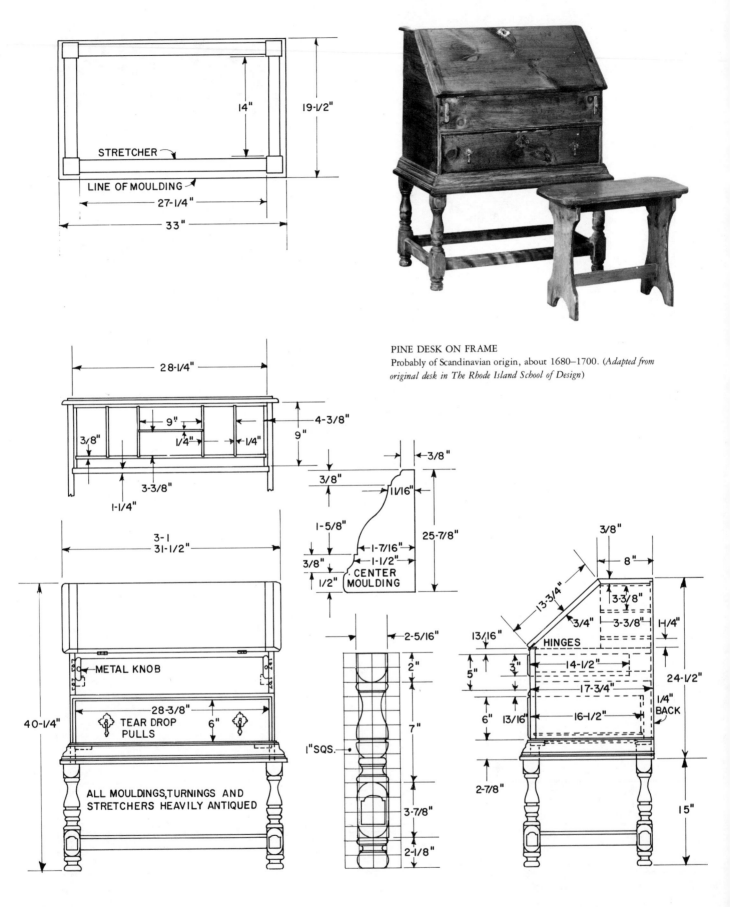

14"

19-1/2"

STRETCHER

LINE OF MOULDING

27-1/4"

33"

PINE DESK ON FRAME

Probably of Scandinavian origin, about 1680–1700. (*Adapted from original desk in The Rhode Island School of Design*)

28-1/4"

4-3/8"

9"

9"

3/8"

1/4"

1/4"

3-3/8"

1-1/4"

3/8"

3/8"

1-1/16"

3/8"

1-5/8"

25-7/8"

1-7/16"

3/8"

1-1/2"

1/2"

CENTER MOULDING

3-1
31-1/2"

2-5/16"

3/8"

8"

13-3/4"

3-3/8"

3/4"

3-3/8"

1/4"

13/16"

HINGES

METAL KNOB

5"

3"

14-1/2"

24-1/2"

28-3/8"

6"

17-3/4"

TEAR DROP PULLS

40-1/4"

2"

6"

13/16"

16-1/2"

1/4" BACK

7"

1" SQS.

3-7/8"

ALL MOULDINGS, TURNINGS AND STRETCHERS HEAVILY ANTIQUED

2-7/8"

15"

2-1/8"

186

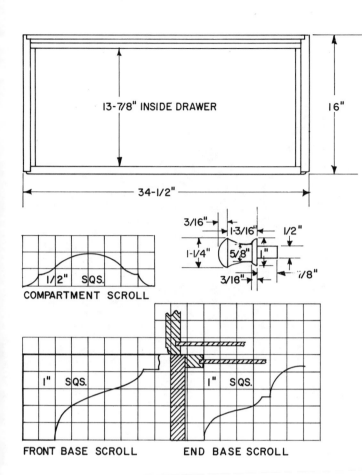

13-7/8" INSIDE DRAWER

16"

34-1/2"

3/16"   1-3/16"   1/2"
1-1/4"   5/8"
3/16"   7/8"

1/2" SQS.

COMPARTMENT SCROLL

1" SQS.   1" SQS.

FRONT BASE SCROLL   END BASE SCROLL

SLANT-FRONT DESK
Probably Virginia, about 1800. (*Adapted from original desk in southern museum*)

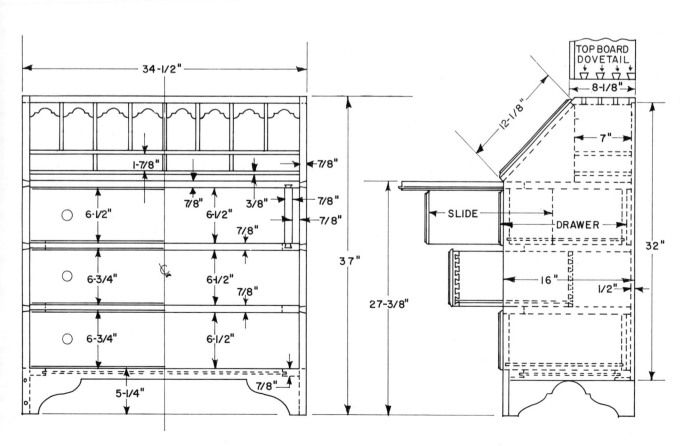

34-1/2"

1-7/8"   7/8"

6-1/2"   7/8"
7/8"   3/8"   7/8"
6-1/2"
7/8"

6-3/4"   6-1/2"   7/8"

37"

6-3/4"   6-1/2"

27-3/8"

5-1/4"   7/8"

TOP BOARD
DOVETAIL

8-1/8"

12-1/8"

7"

SLIDE   DRAWER

32"

16"   1/2"

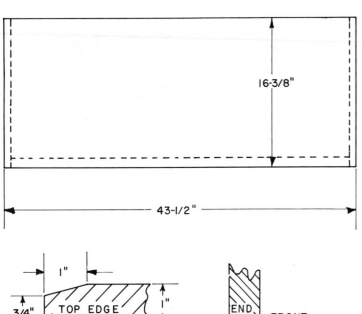

16-3/8"

43-1/2"

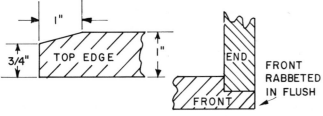

1"

3/4" TOP EDGE 1"

END

FRONT
RABBETED
IN FLUSH

FRONT ← FLUSH

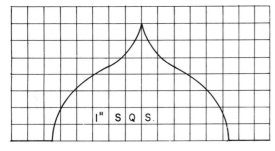

1" SQS.

SIDE FOOT SHAPE

BLANKET CHEST
New England, early 19th century. (*Photographed by author at Fruitlands Museums*)

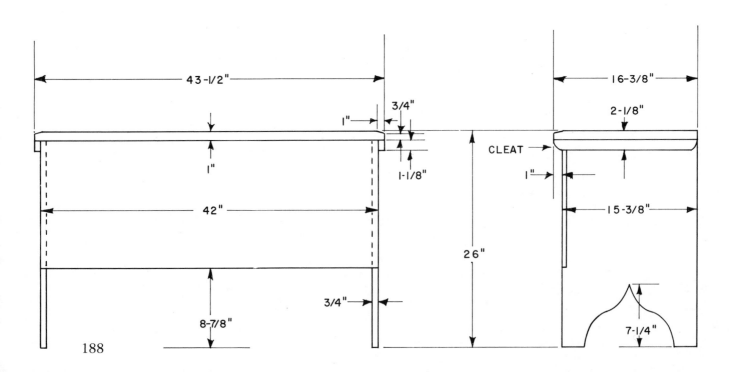

43-1/2"

3/4"

1"

1"

1-1/8"

42"

3/4"

8-7/8"

188

16-3/8"

2-1/8"

CLEAT

1"

15-3/8"

26"

7-1/4"

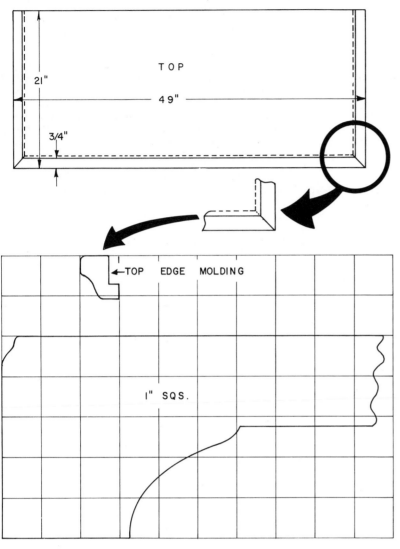

TOP

21"

49"

3/4"

TOP EDGE MOLDING

1" SQS.

CONNECTICUT CHEST
Connecticut, about 1815. (*Photographed by author at Fruitlands Museums*)

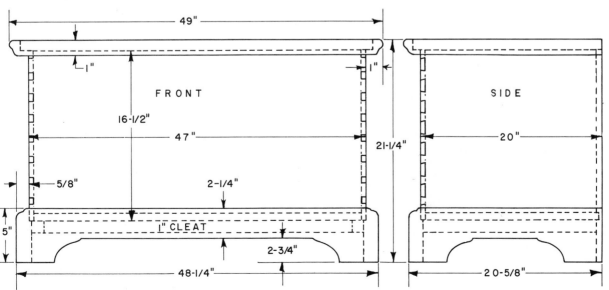

49"

1"

FRONT

16-1/2"

47"

1"

21-1/4"

5/8"

2-1/4"

1" CLEAT

5"

2-3/4"

48-1/4"

SIDE

20"

20-5/8"

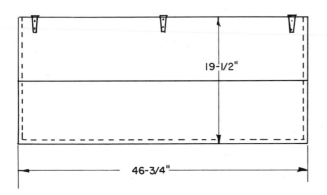

19-1/2"

46-3/4"

FRENCH CANADIAN FOUR-PANELED CHEST
Province of Quebec, Canada, 18th century. (*Photographed by author at The Montreal Museum of Fine Arts*)

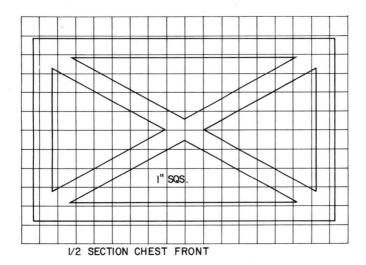

1" SQS.

1/2 SECTION CHEST FRONT

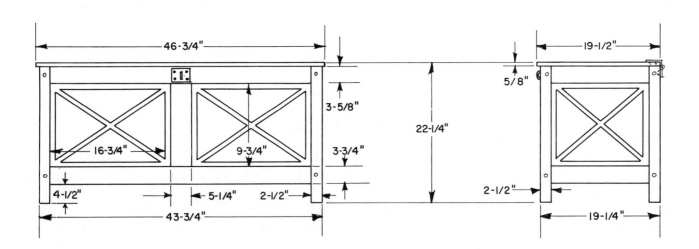

46-3/4"

19-1/2"

5/8"

3-5/8"

22-1/4"

16-3/4"   9-3/4"

3-3/4"

4-1/2"   5-1/4"   2-1/2"

2-1/2"

43-3/4"

19-1/4"

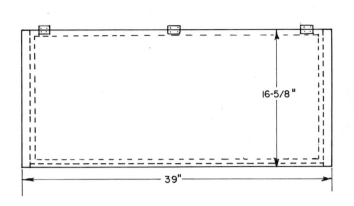

16-5/8"

39"

SPANISH CLOTHING CHEST
Santander, Spain, about 1750. (*Courtesy, Historic St. Augustine Preservation Board*)

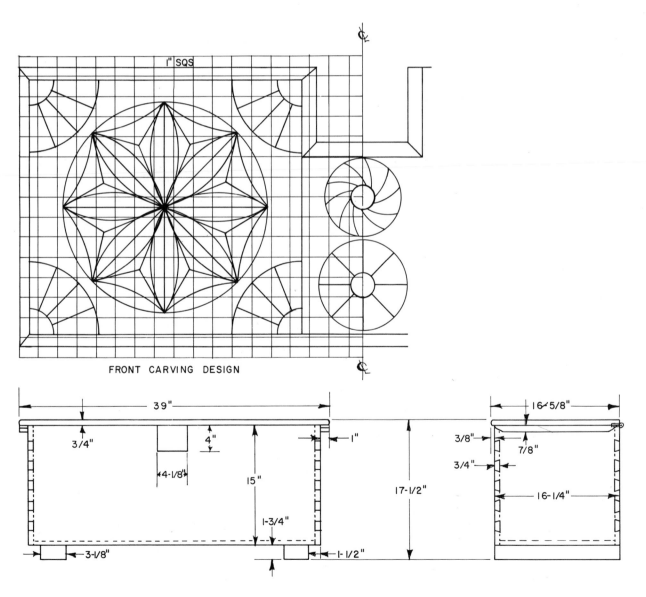

1" SQS

FRONT CARVING DESIGN

39"

3/4"

4"

4-1/8"

15"

1-3/4"

3-1/8"

1"

1-1/2"

16-5/8"

3/8"

7/8"

3/4"

16-1/4"

17-1/2"

191

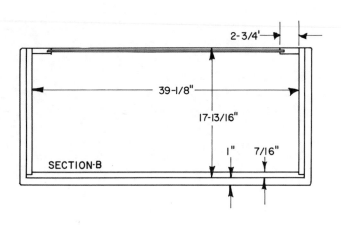

SECTION-B

2-3/4'

39-1/8"

17-13/16"

1"   7/16"

CHEST WITH ONE DRAWER
Massachusetts, late 17th century. (*Reproduced from original in The Old Ironmaster's House, Saugus, Massachusetts*)

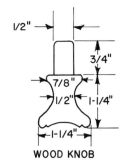

1/2"

3/4"

7/8"

1/2"   1-1/4"

1-1/4"

WOOD KNOB

DOVETAILED   1/2"

7-1/4"   16-1/4"

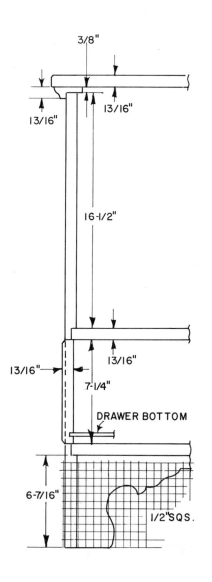

3/8"

13/16"

13/16"

16-1/2"

13/16"

13/16"

7-1/4"

DRAWER BOTTOM

6-7/16"

1/2"SQS.

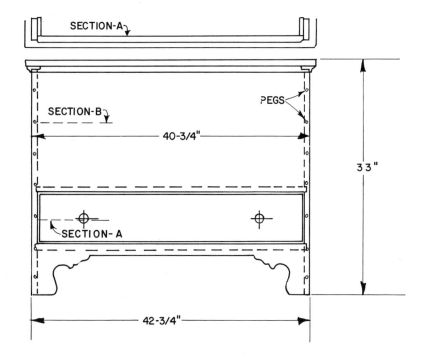

SECTION-A

SECTION-B

PEGS

40-3/4"

33"

SECTION-A

42-3/4"

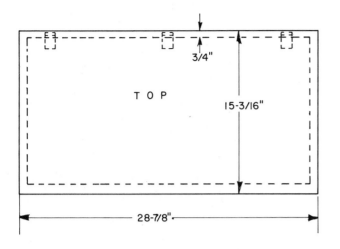

3/4"

TOP

15-3/16"

28-7/8"

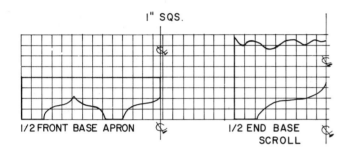

1" SQS.

1/2 FRONT BASE APRON   1/2 END BASE
                              SCROLL

PINE CHEST WITH DRAWER
New England, about 1710. (*Courtesy, Longfellow's Wayside Inn*)

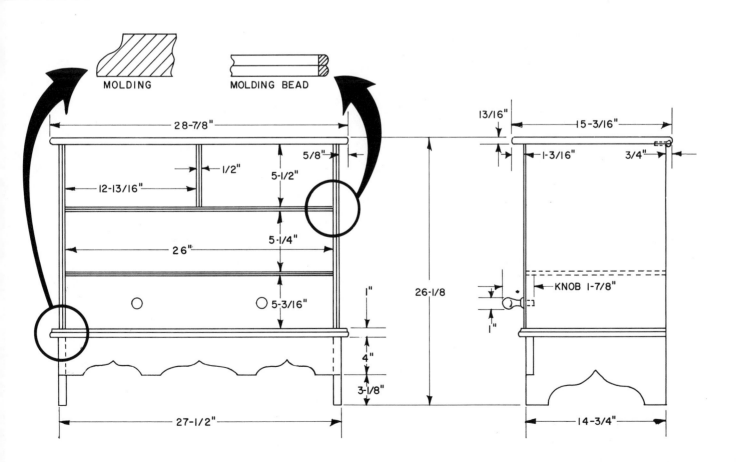

MOLDING   MOLDING BEAD

28-7/8"

5/8"

1/2"

12-13/16"

5-1/2"

26"

5-1/4"

5-3/16"

1"

4"

3-1/8"

27-1/2"

13/16"

15-3/16"

1-3/16"

3/4"

26-1/8

KNOB 1-7/8"

1"

14-3/4"

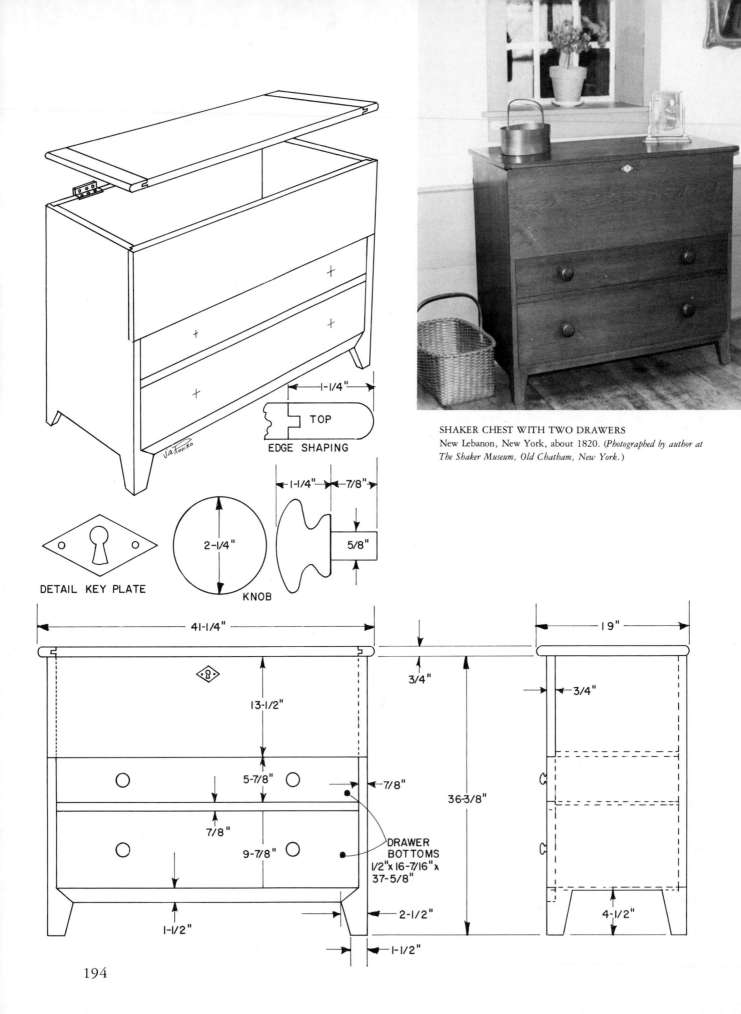

TOP

EDGE SHAPING

1-1/4"

1-1/4"   7/8"

2-1/4"

5/8"

DETAIL KEY PLATE

KNOB

SHAKER CHEST WITH TWO DRAWERS
New Lebanon, New York, about 1820. (*Photographed by author at
The Shaker Museum, Old Chatham, New York.*)

41-1/4"

19"

3/4"

3/4"

13-1/2"

5-7/8"   7/8"

36-3/8"

7/8"

9-7/8"

DRAWER
BOTTOMS
1/2" x 16-7/16" x
37-5/8"

1-1/2"

2-1/2"

4-1/2"

1-1/2"

194

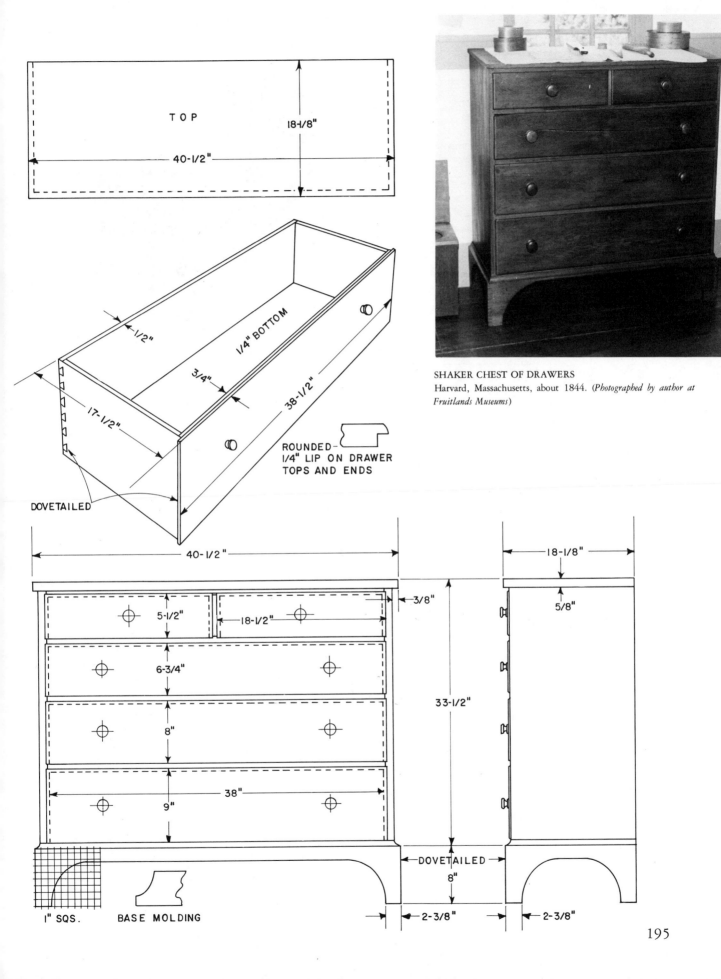

TOP

18-1/8"

40-1/2"

1/2"

1/4" BOTTOM

3/4"

38-1/2"

17-1/2"

ROUNDED
1/4" LIP ON DRAWER
TOPS AND ENDS

DOVETAILED

SHAKER CHEST OF DRAWERS
Harvard, Massachusetts, about 1844. (*Photographed by author at Fruitlands Museums*)

40-1/2"

18-1/8"

3/8"

5/8"

5-1/2"

18-1/2"

6-3/4"

33-1/2"

8"

38"

9"

DOVETAILED

8"

1" SQS.   BASE MOLDING

2-3/8"

2-3/8"

195

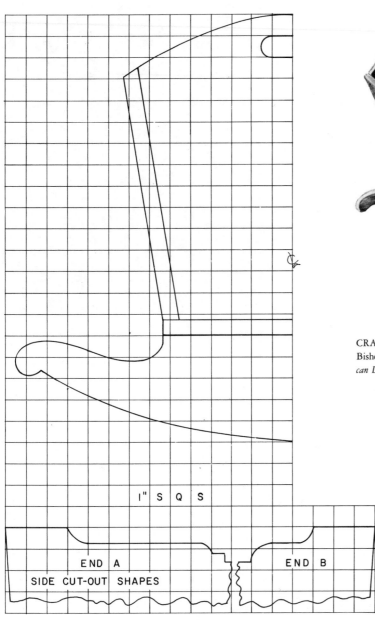

1" S Q S

END A   END B

SIDE CUT-OUT SHAPES

CRADLE
Bishop Hill, Illinois, mid-19th century. (*Courtesy, Index of American Design*)

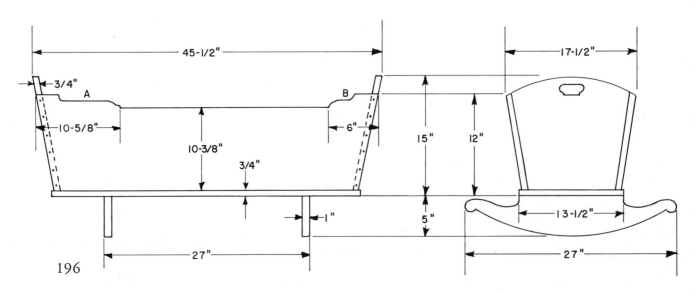

45-1/2"

17-1/2"

3/4"

A   B

10-5/8"   6"

10-3/8"

15"   12"

3/4"

1"   5"

13-1/2"

27"   27"

196

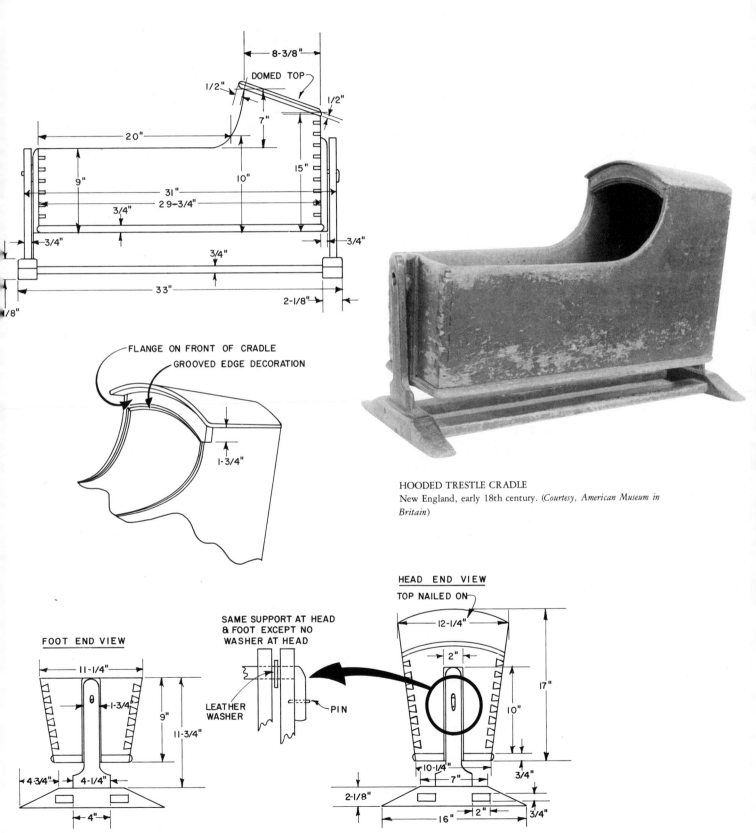

8-3/8"

DOMED TOP

1/2"   1/2"

7"

20"

15"

9"   10"

31"

29-3/4"

3/4"

3/4"   3/4"

3/4"

33"

2-1/8"

1/8"

FLANGE ON FRONT OF CRADLE
GROOVED EDGE DECORATION

1-3/4"

HOODED TRESTLE CRADLE
New England, early 18th century. (*Courtesy, American Museum in Britain*)

FOOT END VIEW

11-1/4"

1-3/4"

9"

11-3/4"

4-3/4"   4-1/4"

4"

SAME SUPPORT AT HEAD
& FOOT EXCEPT NO
WASHER AT HEAD

LEATHER
WASHER   PIN

HEAD END VIEW

TOP NAILED ON

12-1/4"

2"

17"

10"

10-1/4"

7"   3/4"

2-1/8"

16"   2"   3/4"

197

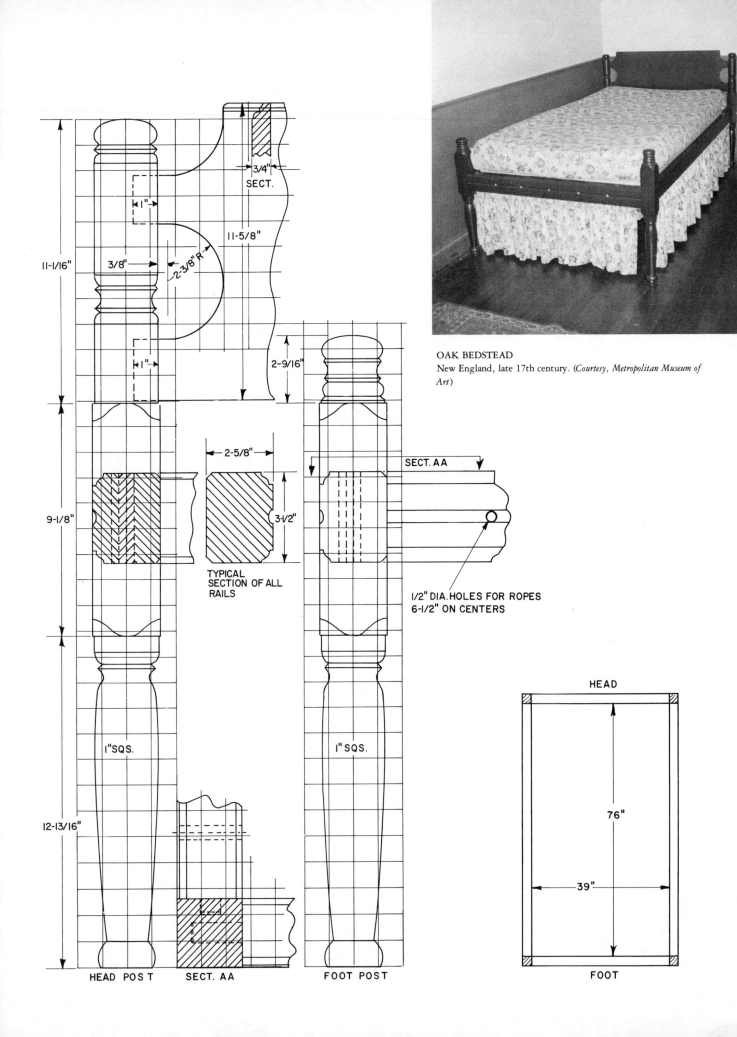

11-1/16"

3/8"

2-3/8" R

11-5/8"

3/4"

SECT.

1"

1"

2-9/16"

9-1/8"

2-5/8"

3-1/2"

TYPICAL
SECTION OF ALL
RAILS

SECT. AA

1/2" DIA. HOLES FOR ROPES
6-1/2" ON CENTERS

1" SQS.

1" SQS.

12-13/16"

HEAD POST

SECT. AA

FOOT POST

OAK BEDSTEAD
New England, late 17th century. (*Courtesy, Metropolitan Museum of Art*)

HEAD

76"

39"

FOOT

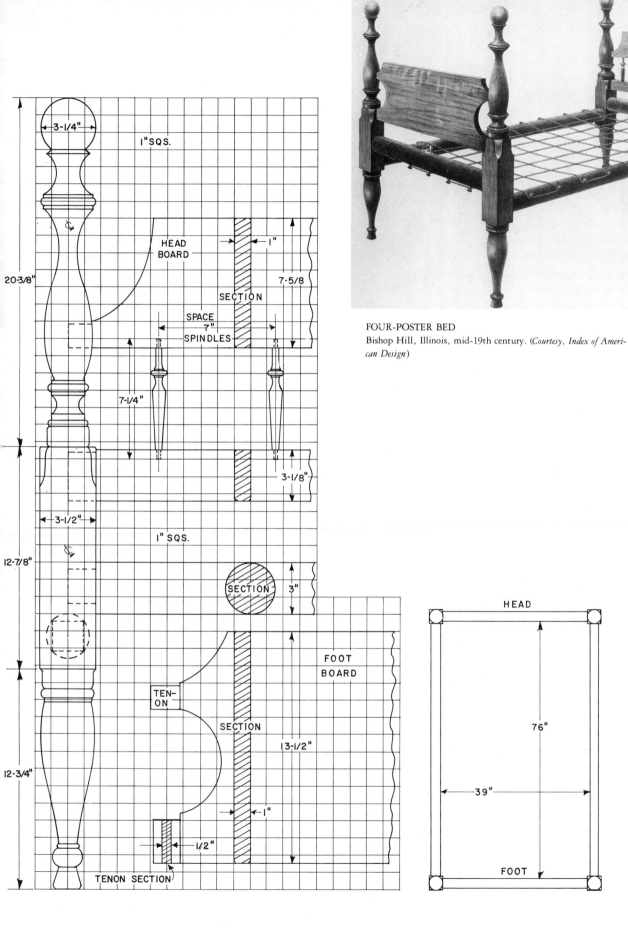

3-1/4"

1" SQS.

20-3/8"

HEAD
BOARD

SECTION

1"

7-5/8"

SPACE
7"
SPINDLES

7-1/4"

3-1/8"

3-1/2"

1" SQS.

12-7/8"

SECTION

3"

FOOT
BOARD

TEN-
ON

SECTION

13-1/2"

12-3/4"

1"

1/2"

TENON SECTION

FOUR-POSTER BED

Bishop Hill, Illinois, mid-19th century. (*Courtesy, Index of American Design*)

HEAD

76"

39"

FOOT

199

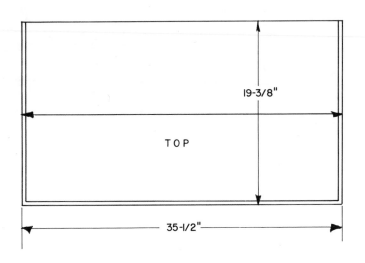

19-3/8"

TOP

35-1/2"

FRENCH CANADIAN SMALL ARMOIRE
Richelieu, Province of Quebec, early 18th century. (*Photographed by author at The Montreal Museum of Fine Arts*)

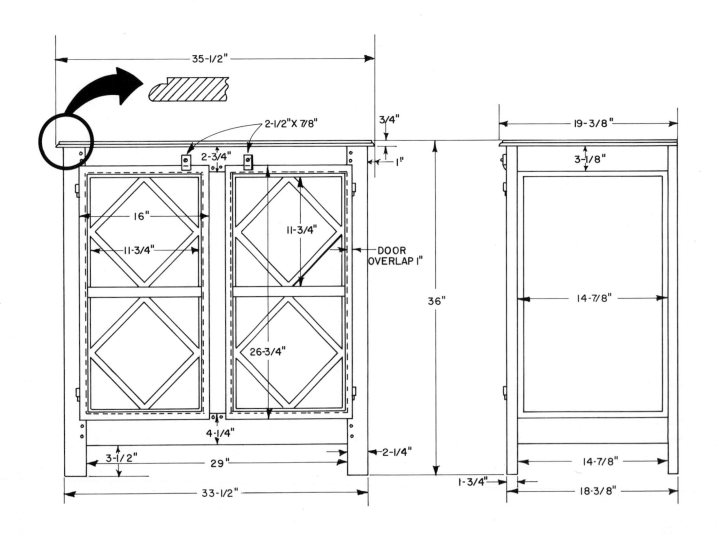

35-1/2"

2-1/2" X 7/8"

3/4"

2-3/4"

19-3/8"

1"

3-1/8"

16"

11-3/4"

11-3/4"

DOOR OVERLAP 1"

14-7/8"

36"

26-3/4"

4-1/4"

3-1/2"

29"

2-1/4"

14-7/8"

33-1/2"

1-3/4"

18-3/8"

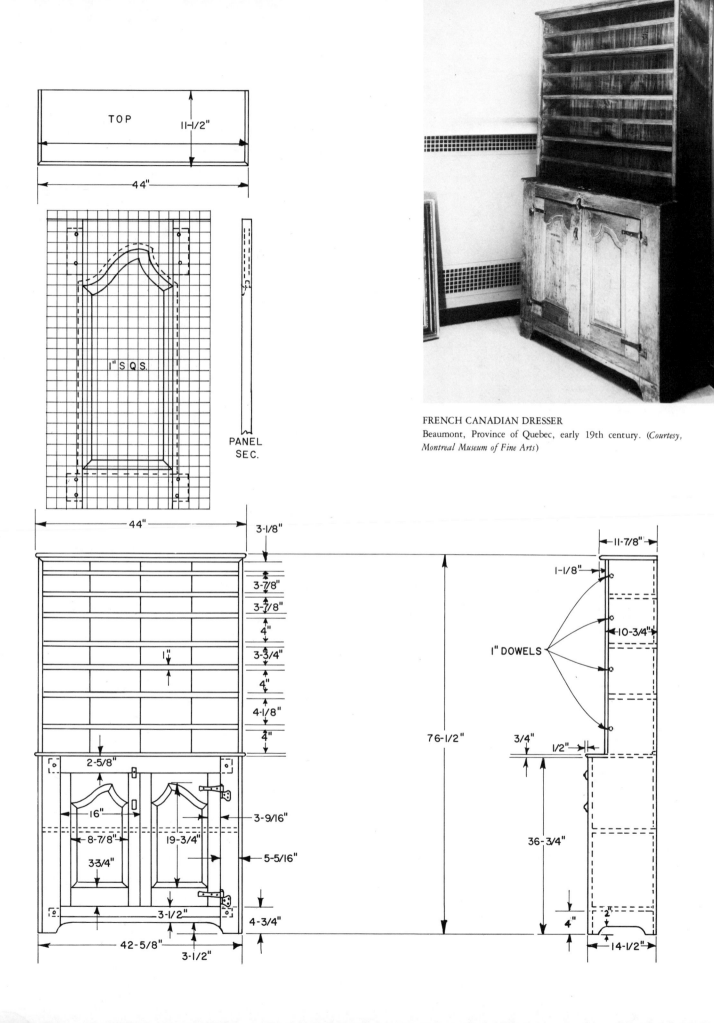

TOP

11-1/2"

44"

1" SQS.

PANEL SEC.

FRENCH CANADIAN DRESSER
Beaumont, Province of Quebec, early 19th century. (*Courtesy, Montreal Museum of Fine Arts*)

44"

3-1/8"

3-7/8"

3-7/8"

4"

3-3/4"

1"

4"

4-1/8"

4"

2-5/8"

16"

3-9/16"

8-7/8"

19-3/4"

5-5/16"

3-3/4"

3-1/2"

4-3/4"

42-5/8"

3-1/2"

11-7/8"

1-1/8"

10-3/4"

1" DOWELS

76-1/2"

3/4"

1/2"

36-3/4"

2"

4"

14-1/2"

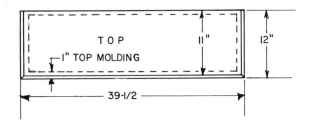

TOP

1" TOP MOLDING

11"

12"

39-1/2

1" S Q S

SECTION

1-7/8"

FOOT DESIGN

SPANISH CUPBOARD
Catalonia, Spain, about 1820. (*Courtesy, Historic St. Augustine Preservation Board*)

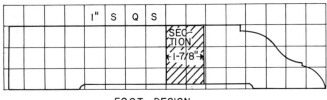

39-1/2"

1-3/4"   1-7/8"

1"

1-5/8"

2-1/4"

28-1/4"

1-3/4"

2-3/16"

3"

1-1/2"

16-1/2"

2-3/4"

29-1/4"

5-3/4"

3"

202

3"

1-7/8"

68-3/16"

5"

11"

3"

15-3/4"

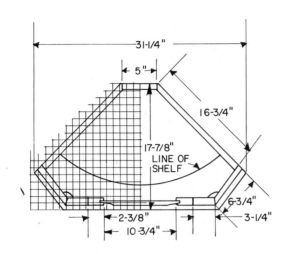

31-1/4"
5"
16-3/4"
17-7/8"
LINE OF SHELF
6-3/4"
2-3/8"
3-1/4"
10-3/4"

PENNSYLVANIA GERMAN CORNER CUPBOARD

Pennsylvania, about 1725. *(Adapted from original in The Philadelphia Museum of Art)*

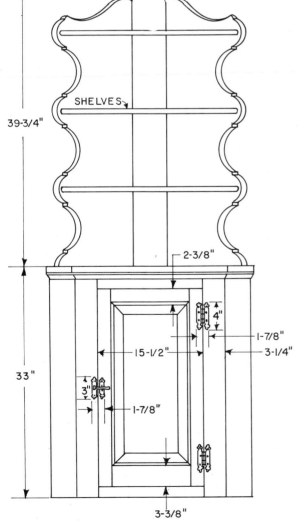

SHELVES

39-3/4"

2-3/8"

4"

1-7/8"

15-1/2"

3-1/4"

33"

3"

1-7/8"

3-3/8"

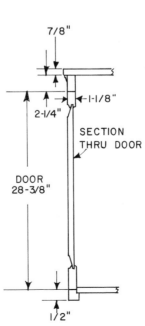

7/8"

1-1/8"

2-1/4"

SECTION THRU DOOR

DOOR 28-3/8"

1/2"

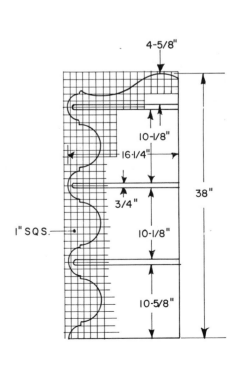

4-5/8"

10-1/8"

16-1/4"

3/4"

1" SQS.

10-1/8"

38"

10-5/8"

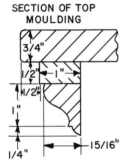

LINE OF UPPER SHELF   LINE OF LOWER SHELF

1-5/8"   3-1/4"

5"   7"

1" SQS.

SECTION OF TOP
MOULDING

MOULDING OF
BACK BOARDS

3/4"

1/2"   1"

1/2"

1"

1/4"   15/16"

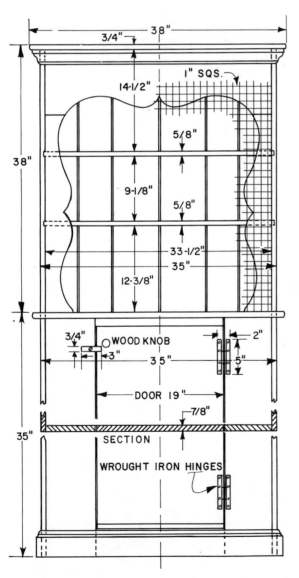

38"

3/4"

1" SQS.

14-1/2"

5/8"

38"

9-1/8"

5/8"

33-1/2"

35"

12-3/8"

3/4"   WOOD KNOB   2"

3"   35"   5"

DOOR 19"

7/8"

35"   SECTION

WROUGHT IRON HINGES

CYMA-SCROLLED CUPBOARD
New England, about 1720–1750. (*Adapted from original in the
Wadsworth Atheneum*)

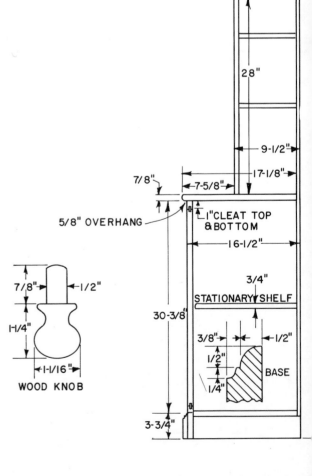

WOOD KNOB

7/8"   1/2"

1-1/4"

1-1/16"

11"

9-1/4"

28"

9-1/2"

17-1/8"

7/8"

7-5/8"

5/8" OVERHANG

1"CLEAT TOP
& BOTTOM

16-1/2"

3/4"

STATIONARY SHELF

3/8"   1/2"

30-3/8"

1/2"

1/4"   BASE

3-3/4"

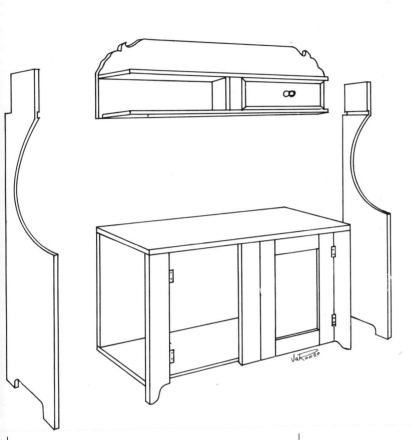

WATER BENCH
New England, about 1700. *(Pen-sketched from original museum model)*

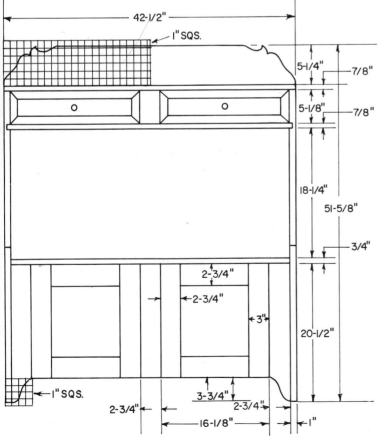

42-1/2"

1" SQS.

5-1/4" 7/8"

5-1/8" 7/8"

18-1/4"

51-5/8"

3/4"

2-3/4"

2-3/4"

3"

20-1/2"

1" SQS.

3-3/4"

2-3/4" 2-3/4"

16-1/8" 1"

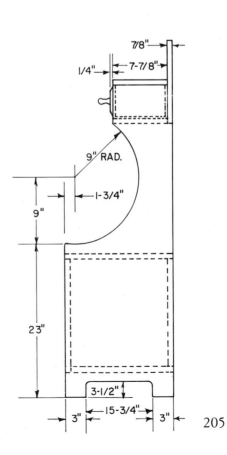

7/8"

7-7/8"

1/4"

9" RAD.

9"

1-3/4"

23"

3-1/2"

3" 15-3/4" 3"

205

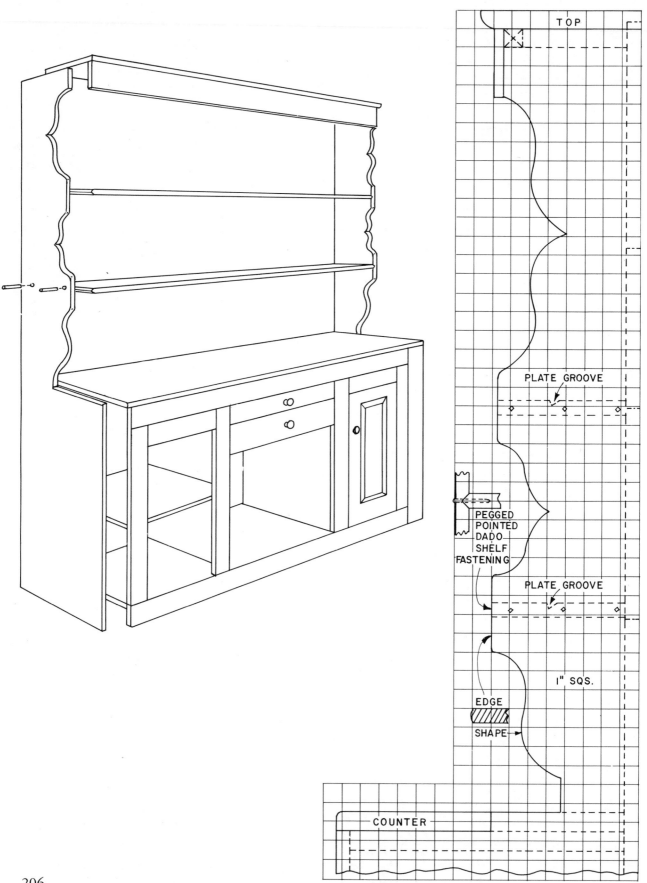

TOP

PLATE GROOVE

PEGGED
POINTED
DADO
SHELF
FASTENING

PLATE GROOVE

1" SQS.

EDGE

SHAPE

COUNTER

PINE DRESSER

New England, about 1740–1780. This handsome old dresser stands at the back wall of the kitchen in the restored inn, featured in Longfellow's *"Tales of a Wayside Inn."* (*Courtesy, Longfellow's Wayside Inn*)

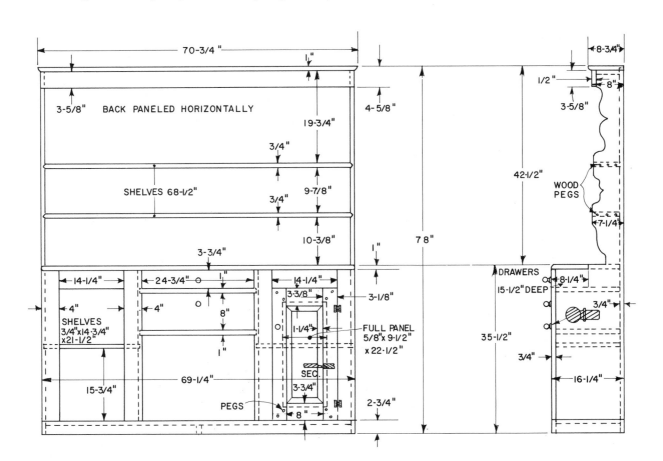

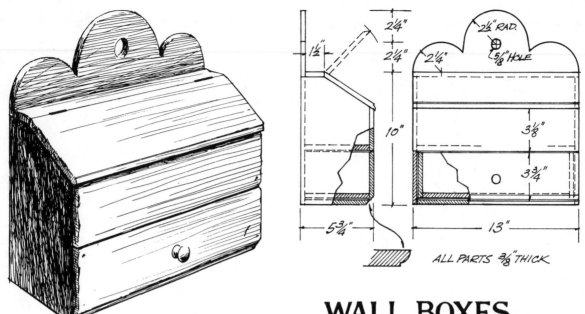

2¼"
2¼"
1½"
10"
5¾"

2½" RAD.
5/8" HOLE
2¼"
2¼"
3⅛"
3¾"
13"

ALL PARTS ⅜" THICK

WALL BOXES,
BRACKETS & SCONCES

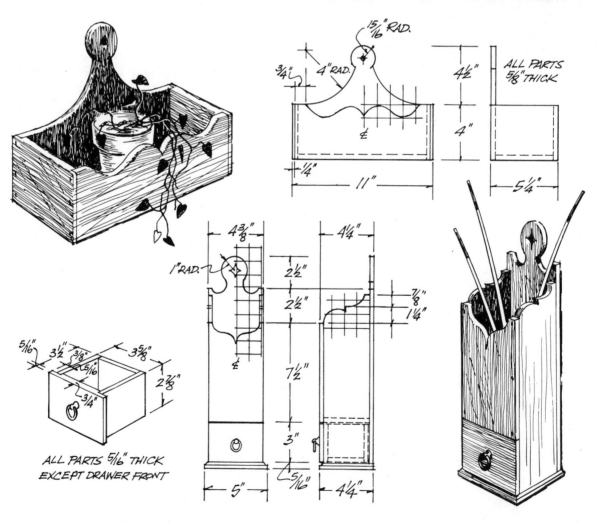

15/16" RAD.
4" RAD.
¾"
¼"
11"
4½"
4"
5¼"
ALL PARTS ⅝" THICK

5/16"
3½"
3/8"
3⅝"
5/16"
2⅞"
¾"
ALL PARTS 5/16" THICK
EXCEPT DRAWER FRONT

1" RAD.
4⅜"
2½"
2½"
7½"
3"
5/16"
5"

4¼"
7/8"
1¼"
4¼"

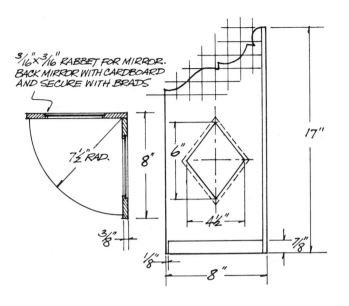

³⁄₁₆" × ³⁄₁₆" RABBET FOR MIRROR.
BACK MIRROR WITH CARDBOARD
AND SECURE WITH BRADS

7½" RAD.

8"

6"

4½"

17"

⅞"

⅛"

⅜"

8"

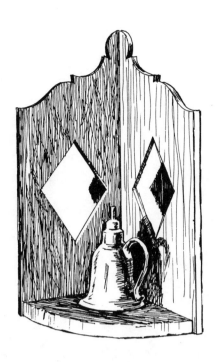

Antique country furniture abounds with quaint items produced by early American craftsmen over two hundred years ago. From museums and private collections come the appealing little antiques sketched on these pages. All are authentic. The pine wall boxes held cutlery and tallow candles; the pipe box, the master's long-stemmed pipes. The wooden candle sconces and the pine bracket lantern are used today for electric lights, adapting colonial craftsmanship to contemporary living.

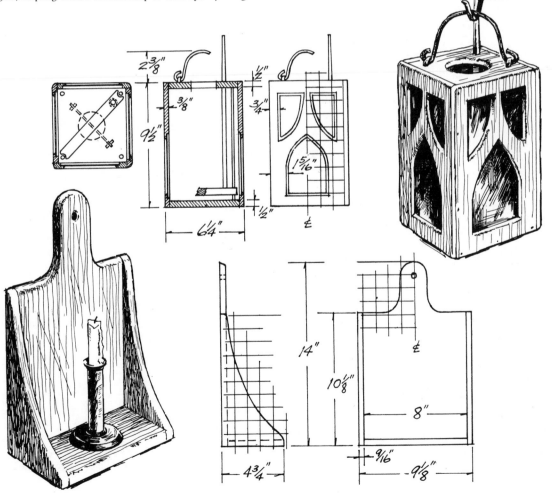

2³⁄₈"

3⁄₈"

9½"

6¼"

½"

½"

¾"

1⁵⁄₁₆"

¢

14"

10⅛"

8"

4¾"

9⁄₁₆"

9⅛"

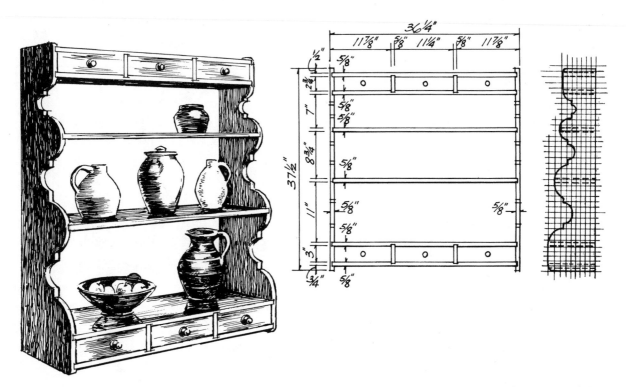

WALL RACKS & SHELVES

The craftsmen among our colonial forefathers were particularly inventive in their construction of wall shelves and utility racks. Many graceful designs of both large and small "sets of shelves" (as they were originally called) may now be found in our museums. The examples shown on these pages are among the most interesting and ingenious. They are all of 17th and early 18th century origin. The wood used was soft pine. Exposed dado and dovetail joints reveal typically honest construction.

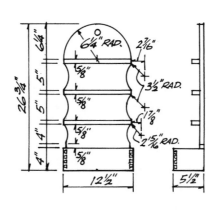

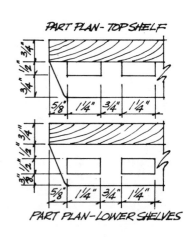

PART PLAN – TOP SHELF

PART PLAN – LOWER SHELVES

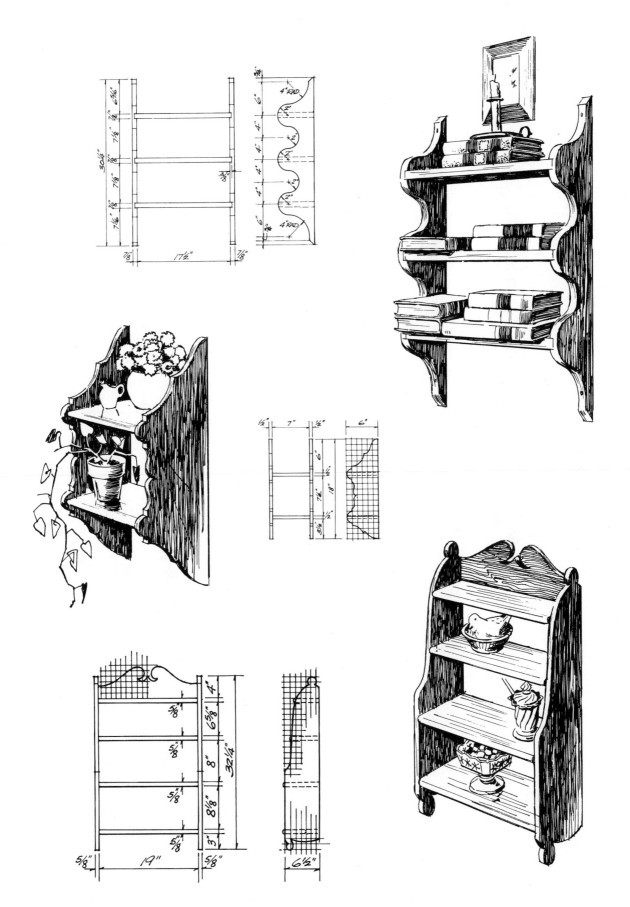

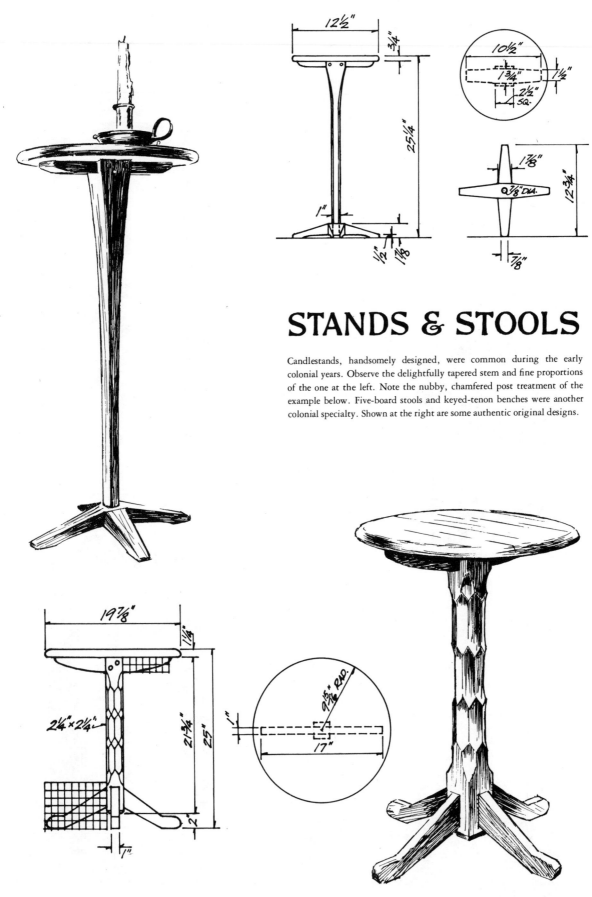

STANDS & STOOLS

Candlestands, handsomely designed, were common during the early colonial years. Observe the delightfully tapered stem and fine proportions of the one at the left. Note the nubby, chamfered post treatment of the example below. Five-board stools and keyed-tenon benches were another colonial specialty. Shown at the right are some authentic original designs.

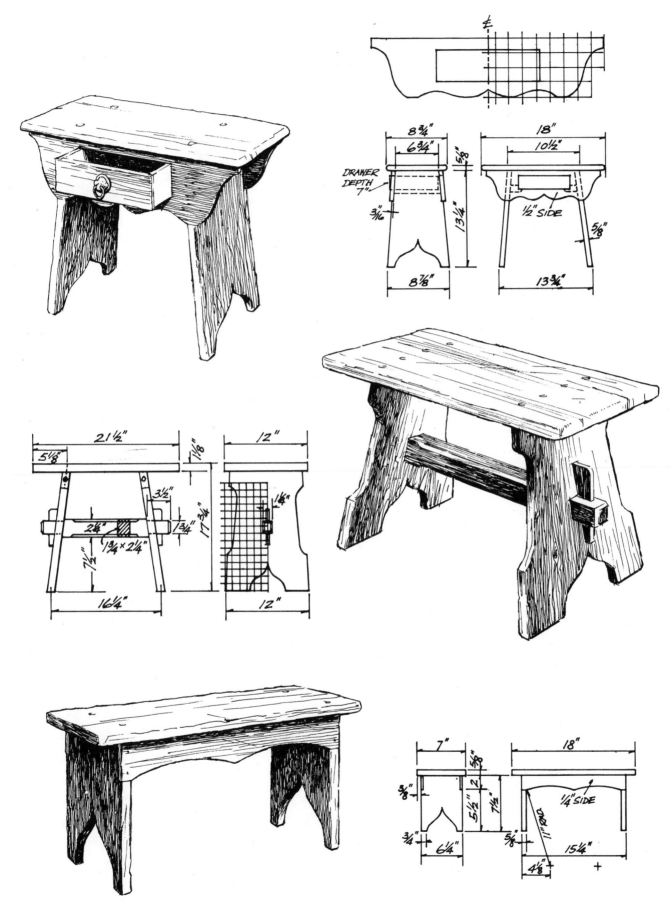

8 3/4"
6 3/4"
5/8"
DRAWER
DEPTH
7"
3/16"
13 1/4"
8 7/8"

18"
10 1/2"
1/2" SIDE
5/8"
13 3/4"

21 1/2"
5 1/8"
1/8"
3 1/2"
2 1/4"
1 3/4" × 2 1/4"
1 3/4"
17 3/4"
7 1/2"
16 1/4"

12"
1/8"
12"

7"
5/8"
2"
3/8"
5 1/2"
7 1/2"
3/4"
6 1/4"
5/8"

18"
1/4" SIDE
1
1" RAD
4/8"
15 1/4"

PEG-LEG PERSONALITIES

6"

3½"

1" WEDGED TENON

15"

TYPICAL

45°

45"

EDGE SHAPE

1¾"

15¼"

CHAMFER
⅜" TO 0"

1¾"

15"

3"

3"

10"

2 1" WEDGED
TENON

EDGE SHAPE

1¾"

14"

CHAMFER
⅜" TO 0"

1¾"

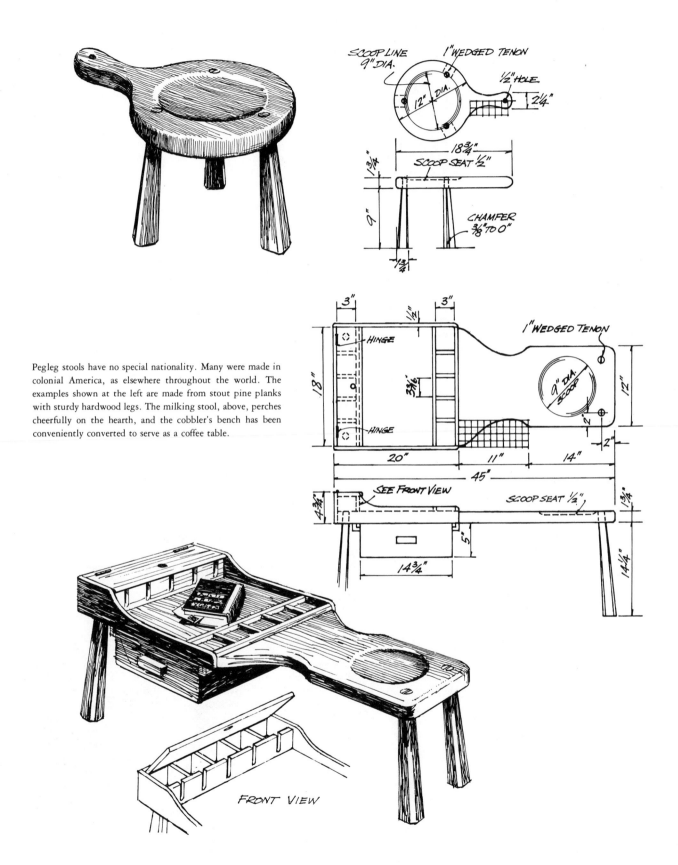

SCOOP LINE 9" DIA.

1" WEDGED TENON

1/2" HOLE

2 1/4"

12" DIA.

18 3/4"

1 3/4"

SCOOP SEAT 1/2"

9"

1 3/4"

CHAMFER 3/8" TO 0"

Pegleg stools have no special nationality. Many were made in colonial America, as elsewhere throughout the world. The examples shown at the left are made from stout pine planks with sturdy hardwood legs. The milking stool, above, perches cheerfully on the hearth, and the cobbler's bench has been conveniently converted to serve as a coffee table.

3"

1/2"

3"

1" WEDGED TENON

HINGE

18"

3 3/16"

9" DIA. SCOOP

12"

HINGE

2"

2"

20"

11"

14"

45"

SEE FRONT VIEW

SCOOP SEAT 1/2"

1 3/4"

4 3/4"

5"

14 1/4"

14 3/4"

FRONT VIEW

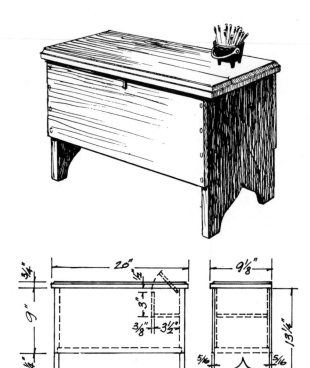

SIX-BOARD CHEST
New England, about 1700. *(Pen-sketched from photograph)*

WATER BENCH
Pennsylvania, about 1720. *(Pen-sketched from photograph)*

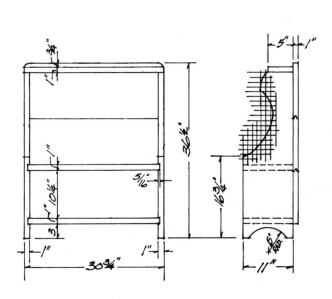

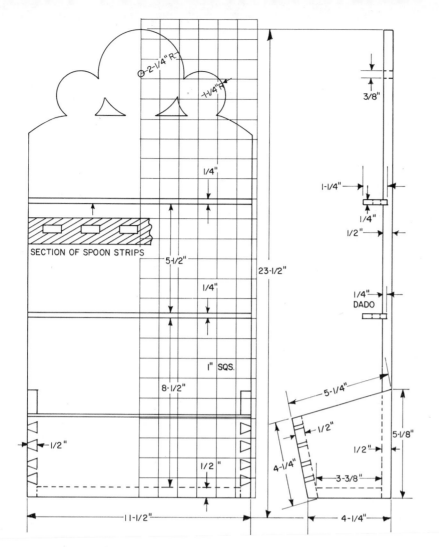

SECTION OF SPOON STRIPS

SPOON RACK
New York or New England, about 1750. (*Photographed by author at Sleepy Hollow Restorations*)

WALL BOX
New England, early 18th century. (*Photographed by author at Sleepy Hollow Restorations*)

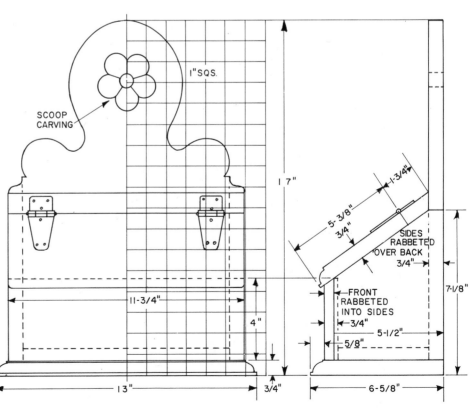

SCOOP CARVING

1" SQS.

SIDES RABBETED OVER BACK

FRONT RABBETED INTO SIDES

217

Selected Bibliography

Albers, Marjorie K., OLD AMANA FURNITURE, Locust House, Shenandoah, Iowa.

Andrews, Edward D., THE PEOPLE CALLED SHAKERS, Dover, New York.

———— and Faith, RELIGION IN WOOD, Indiana University Press, Bloomington.

————, SHAKER FURNITURE, Dover, New York.

BALTIMORE FURNITURE 1760–1810. Baltimore Museum of Art, Baltimore.

Beneat, Paul, LE MOBILIER BRETON, Massin, Paris.

Benn, R. D., STYLE IN FURNITURE, Longmans Green, London.

Bishop, Robert, THE AMERICAN CHAIR; HOW TO KNOW ANTIQUE FURNITURE, Dutton, New York.

Bjerkoe, Ethel Hall, THE CABINETMAKERS OF AMERICA, Doubleday, New York.

Boyd, E., POPULAR ARTS OF SPANISH NEW MEXICO, Museum of New Mexico, Santa Fe.

Brand, Millen, FIELDS OF PEACE — A PENNSYLVANIA GERMAN ALBUM, Doubleday, New York.

Brinton, C., Chistopher, J. and Wolff, R. L., A HISTORY OF CIVILIZATION, Prentice-Hall, Englewood Cliffs, New Jersey.

Brown, Charles H., VAN CORTLANDT MANOR, Sleepy Hollow Restorations, Tarrytown, New York.

Burroughs, Paul H., SOUTHERN ANTIQUES, Crown, New York.

Butler, Joseph T., AMERICAN ANTIQUES 1800–1900, Odyssey, New York.

————, AMERICAN FURNITURE, Triune, London.

Castedo, Leopold, A HISTORY OF LATIN AMERICAN ART & ARCHITECTURE FROM PRE-COLUMBIAN TIMES TO THE PRESENT, Praeger, New York.

Cecinsky, H. and Hunter, G. L., ENGLISH AND AMERICAN FURNITURE, Dean-Hicks, New York.

Clark, Thomas P. and Ham, F. Gerald, PLEASANT HILL AND ITS SHAKERS, Shakertown, Pleasant Hill, Kentucky.

Clouzot, Henri, LES MEUBLE DU XVIIIE SIÈCLE, Morance, Paris.

Cole, Herbert, AN INTRODUCTION TO THE PERIOD STYLES OF ENGLAND AND FRANCE, Sutherland, Manchester, England.

Comstock, Helen, AMERICAN FURNITURE, Viking, New York.

————, 100 MOST BEAUTIFUL ROOMS IN AMERICA, Viking, New York.

————, CONCISE ENCYCLOPEDIA OF AMERICAN ANTIQUES (2 vols.), Hawthorn, New York.

Cooke, Alistair, AMERICA, Knopf, New York.

Cornelius, C. O., EARLY AMERICAN FURNITURE, Appleton-Century, New York.

Damay, Paul F., ART IN LATIN AMERICAN ARCHITECTURE, Reinhold, New York.

Davidson, Marshall B., HISTORY OF NOTABLE AMERICAN HOUSES, American Heritage, New York.

Dilliard, Maud Esther, AN ALBUM OF NEW NETHERLAND, Bramhall House, New York.

Dow, George Francis, THE ARTS AND CRAFTS OF NEW ENGLAND 1704–1775, Wayside, Topsfield, Massachusetts.

Downs, Joseph, PICTURE BOOK OF THE AMERICAN WING, Metropolitan Museum of Art, New York.

Dreppard, Carl W., HANDBOOK OF AMERICAN CHAIRS, Doubleday, New York.

Dreyfus, Carle, LE MOBILIER FRANÇAIS (2 vols.), Morance, Paris.

Durant, Mary, AMERICAN HERITAGE GUIDE TO ANTIQUES, American Heritage, New York.

Eberlein, Harold Donaldson, THE PRACTICAL BOOK OF ITALIAN, SPANISH AND PORTUGESE FURNITURE, Lippincott, Philadelphia.

———— and McClure, Abbot, THE PRACTICAL BOOK OF PERIOD FURNITURE, Lippincott, Philadelphia.

Fales, Dean A., Jr., ESSEX COUNTY FURNITURE, Essex Institute, Salem, Massachusetts.

————, and Bishop, R., AMERICAN PAINTED FURNITURE 1660–1880, Dutton, New York.

Fastnedge, Ralph, ENGLISH FURNITURE STYLES 1500 TO 1836. Barnes, Cranbury, New Jersey.

Felice, Roger de, FRENCH FURNITURE UNDER LOUIS XV, Stokes, New York.

Gould, G. G. and F., THE PERIOD FURNITURE HANDBOOK, Dodd, Mead, New York.

Gloag, John, THE CHAIR: ITS ORIGINS, DESIGN AND SOCIAL HISTORY, Barnes, Cranbury, New Jersey.

GREENFIELD VILLAGE AND THE HENRY FORD MUSEUM (3 vols.), Crown, New York.

Hafen, L. R. and Rister, Carl C., WESTERN AMERICA, Prentice-Hall, Englewood Cliffs, New Jersey.

Halsey, R. T. H., A HANDBOOK OF THE AMERICAN WING OPENING EXHIBITION, Metropolitan Museum of Art, New York.

———— and Tower, E., THE HOMES OF OUR ANCESTORS, Doubleday, New York.

Hayden, Arthur, CHATS ON OLD FURNITURE, Stokes, New York.

Hinckley, F. Lewis, A DIRECTORY OF ANTIQUE FURNITURE, Crown, New York.

———, DIRECTORY OF HISTORIC CABINET WOODS, Crown, New York.

Hofstadter, Richard, Miller, William and Aaron, Daniel, THE UNITED STATES, Prentice-Hall, Englewood Cliffs, New Jersey.

Hornung, Clarence P., TREASURY OF AMERICAN DESIGN, Abrams, New York.

Hutton, Daniel Mac-Hir, OLD SHAKERTOWN AND THE SHAKERS, Harrodsburg Herald, Harrodsburg, Kentucky.

Iverson, Marion Day, THE AMERICAN CHAIR 1630–1890, Hastings House, New York.

Kenney, John Tarrant, THE HITCHCOCK CHAIR, Potter, New York.

Kettell, Russell Hawes, THE PINE FURNITURE OF EARLY NEW ENGLAND, Dover, New York.

Kirk, John T. and Maynard, Henry P., CONNECTICUT FURNITURE — SEVENTEENTH AND EIGHTEENTH CENTURIES, Wadsworth Atheneum, Hartford.

———, EARLY AMERICAN FURNITURE: HOW TO RECOGNIZE, BUY AND CARE FOR THE MOST BEAUTIFUL PIECES — HIGH STYLE, COUNTRY, PRIMITIVE AND RUSTIC, Knopf, New York.

Klamkin, Marian, HANDS TO WORK, Dodd, Mead, New York.

Kovel, Ralph and Terry, AMERICAN COUNTRY FURNITURE, Crown, New York.

Kubler, George and Sona, Marie, ART AND ARCHITECTURE IN SPAIN AND PORTUGAL AND THEIR AMERICAN DOMINIONS 1500–1800, Penguin, Baltimore.

Le Clerc, Leon, LE MOBILIER NORMAND. Massin, Paris.

Lichten, Frances, FOLK ART OF RURAL PENNSYLVANIA, Scribner, New York.

Litchfield, Frederick, ILLUSTRATED HISTORY OF FURNITURE, Truelove Adams, London.

Lockwood, Luke Vincent, COLONIAL FURNITURE IN AMERICA, Castle, New York.

Lockwood, Sarah M., ANTIQUES, Doubleday, New York.

Longnon, H. A. and Huard, F. W., FRENCH PROVINCIAL FURNITURE, Lippincott, Philadelphia.

Lyon, I. W., COLONIAL FURNITURE OF NEW ENGLAND, Houghton Mifflin, Boston.

Meader, Robert F. W., CATALOG OF THE EMMA B. KING LIBRARY OF THE SHAKER MUSEUM, Shaker Museum Foundation, Old Chatham, New York.

———, ILLUSTRATED GUIDE TO SHAKER FURNITURE, Dover, New York.

Melcher, Marguerite Fellows, THE SHAKER ADVENTURE, Case Western Reserve, Cleveland.

THE METROPOLITAN MUSEUM OF ART GUIDE TO THE COLLECTIONS: THE AMERICAN WING, Metropolitan Museum of Art, New York.

THE METROPOLITAN MUSEUM OF ART PENNSYLVANIA GERMAN ARTS AND CRAFTS, Metropolitan Museum of Art, New York.

Miller, Edgar G., Jr., AMERICAN ANTIQUE FURNITURE, Dover, New York.

Moore, N. H., THE OLD FURNITURE BOOK, Stokes, New York.

Newcomb, Rexford, THE OLD MISSION CHURCHES, Lippincott, Philadelphia.

Nutting, Wallace, FURNITURE OF THE PILGRIM CENTURY (2 vols.), Dover, New York.

Ormsbee, Thomas H., FIELD GUIDE TO EARLY AMERICAN FURNITURE, Little Brown, Boston.

Osburn, Burl N., MEASURED DRAWINGS OF EARLY AMERICAN FURNITURE, Bruce, Milwaukee.

Palardy, Jean, THE EARLY FURNITURE OF FRENCH CANADA, MacMillan, Toronto.

Phillips, Hazel Spencer, SHAKERS IN THE WEST, Philadelphia Museum of Art, Philadelphia.

———, TRADITIONAL ARCHITERTURE OF WARREN COUNTY, OHIO. Civic Trust of Lebanon, Ohio.

QUEBEC FURNITURE, National Museum of Man, Ottawa.

Ricci, Seymour de, LOUIS XVI FURNITURE, Putnam, New York.

Rienits, Rex and Thea, THE VOYAGES OF COLUMBUS, Hamlyn, New York.

Ritz, Gislind M., THE ART OF PAINTED FURNITURE, Van Nostrand Reinhold, New York.

Robacker, Earl F., PENNSYLVANIA DUTCH STUFF, Barnes, Cranbury, New Jersey.

Robertson, Donald, PRE-COLUMBIAN ARCHITECTURE, Braziller, New York.

Sack, Albert, FINE POINTS OF FURNITURE: EARLY AMERICAN, Crown, New York.

Sack, Israel, AMERICAN ANTIQUES FROM THE ISRAEL SACK COLLECTION, Highland House, Washington, D.C.

Saglio, André, FRENCH FURNITURE, Scribner, New York.

Schwartz, Mervin D., COUNTRY STYLE, Brooklyn Museum, New York.

THE SHAKERS: THEIR ARTS AND CRAFTS (Bulletin LVII, No. 273), Philadelphia Museum of Art, Philadelphia.

Shea, John G., THE AMERICAN SHAKERS AND THEIR FURNITURE, Van Nostrand Reinhold, New York.

———, COLONIAL FURNITURE MAKING FOR EVERYBODY, Van Nostrand Reinhold, New York.

Singleton, Esther, FURNITURE OF OUR FOREFATHERS, Doubleday, New York.

Slivka, Rose (ed.), THE CRAFTS OF THE MODERN WORLD, Bramhall House, New York.

Staurianos, L. S., THE WORLD SINCE 1500, Prentice-Hall, Englewood Cliffs, New Jersey.

Stewart, J. Douglas and Wilson, Ian E., HERITAGE KINGSTON, Queens University, Kingston.

Stoudt, John Joseph, EARLY PENNSYLVANIA ARTS AND CRAFTS, Barnes, Cranbury, New Jersey.

Sweeney, John A. H., WINTERTHUR ILLUSTRATED, Winterthur Museum, Winterthur, Delaware.

Taylor, H. H., KNOWING, COLLECTING AND RESTORING EARLY AMERICAN FURNITURE, Lippincott, Philadelphia.

Taylor, Lon and Warren, David B., AN INTRODUCTION TO TEXAS FURNITURE, Austin, Texas.

Tunis, Edwin, COLONIAL LIVING, World, Cleveland.

White, Margaret E., EARLY FURNITURE MADE IN NEW JERSEY 1690–1870, Newark Museum, Newark.

Whitehall, Walter Muir, SPANISH ROMANESQUE ARCHITECTURE, Oxford, New York.

Williams, Henry L., COUNTRY FURNITURE OF EARLY AMERICA, Barnes, Cranbury, New Jersey.

——— and Ottalie K., OLD AMERICAN HOUSES 1700–1850, Coward, New York.

Williams, John S., THE SHAKER MUSEUM, Shaker Museum Foundation, Old Chatham, New York.

Williamson, Scott Graham, THE AMERICAN CRAFTSMAN, Bramhall House, New York.

Winchester, Alice, THE ANTIQUES TREASURY, Dutton, New York.

———, HOW TO KNOW AMERICAN ANTIQUES. Signet, New York.

———, LIVING WITH ANTIQUES, Dutton, New York.

Index